GW00339163

The Call and the Commission

The Call and
The Commission

*The challenge of how the Church equips a new
generation of leaders for a different world*

Edited by
ROB FROST, DAVID WILKINSON and JOANNE COX

MILTON KEYNES • COLORADO SPRINGS • HYDERABAD

Copyright © 2009 Rob Frost, David Wilkinson and Joanne Cox

15 14 13 12 11 10 09   7 6 5 4 3 2 1

First published 2009 by Paternoster
Paternoster is an imprint of Authentic Media
9 Holdom Avenue, Bletchley, Milton Keynes, Bucks, MK1 1QR, UK
1820 Jet Stream Drive, Colorado Springs, CO 80921, USA
Medchal Road, Jeedimetla Village, Secunderabad 500 055, A.P., India
www.authenticmedia.co.uk

Paternoster is a division of IBS-STL U.K., limited by guarantee, with its
Registered Office at Kingstown Broadway, Carlisle, Cumbria CA3 0HA.
Registered in England & Wales No. 1216232. Registered charity 270162

The right of Rob Frost, David Wilkinson and Joanne Cox to be identified as the Editors
of this Work has been asserted by them in accordance with the Copyright, Designs and
Patents Act 1988.

*All rights reserved. No part of this publication may be reproduced, stored in a retrieval system,
or transmitted in any form or by any means, electronic, mechanical, photocopying, recording
or otherwise, without the prior permission of the publisher or a licence permitting restricted
copying. In the UK such licences are issued by the Copyright Licensing Agency, 90 Tottenham
Court Road, London, W1P 9HE*

British Library Cataloguing in Publication Data
A catalogue record for this book is available from the British Library

ISBN 978–1–84227–608–2

Cover Design by James Kessel for Scratch the Sky Ltd. (www.scratchthesky.com)
Print Management by Adare
Typeset by Waverley Typesetters, Fakenham
Printed and bound in Great Britain by J.H. Haynes & Co., Sparkford

For Rob

With our thanks

Contents

The Thread

Something is very gently
invisibly, silently,
pulling at me – a thread
or net of threads
finer than cobweb and as
elastic. I haven't tried
the strength of it. No barbed hook
pierced and tore me. Was it
not long ago this thread
began to draw me? Or
way back? Was I
born with its knot about my neck, a bridle? Not fear
but a stirring
of wonder makes me
catch my breath when I feel
the tug of it when I thought
it had loosened itself and gone.

Denise Levertov (*Selected Poems*)

About the Contributors

Martyn Atkins is a Methodist minister currently serving as General Secretary of the Methodist Church of Great Britain. He was President of the Methodist Conference 2007–8 and Principal of Cliff College. He is author of *Resourcing Renewal: Shaping Churches for the Emerging Future* and *Preaching in a Cultural Context*. He is married with three grown sons.

Rev Dr Peter Brierley was Executive Director of Christian Research and MARC Europe for 24 years, and originator of the *UK Christian Handbook* and *Religious Trends*. He writes from this overview of the Church situation in the UK and numerous research assignments in this period. He is currently acting as a consultant to churches and Christian organizations.

Gordon Cotterill lives in London, England, is married to Kate and has two daughters Bethan and Eryn. He has been a Salvation Army officer for nine years and 'cut his teeth' in ministry with his wife as the corps officers at Poplar in the inner city of the East End of London. The lessons he learned there in his day-to-day ministry, amid the chaos of the inner city, continue to shape his understanding and passion for biblical and grace-centred mission. His latest appointment as Spiritual Programme Director at William Booth College, London now offers him the opportunity for the fusion and exploration of 'mission' and 'spiritual formation' while trying to inspire a new generation of Salvation Army officers as to their role in God's plan for His creation. www.urbanarmy. blogspot.com is Gordon's blog where he mulls over themes of mostly mission and spiritual formation.

xii   *The Call and the Commission*

Joanne Cox is a Methodist minister in the Rotherham and Dearne Valley Circuit. She is currently studying for a DMin at Durham University looking at leadership in Fresh Expressions and the influence of Methodist theology. Her working experience includes working in a medical practice, the British Red Cross and serving on a market stall. She is passionate about hospitality, Doctor Who and the cinema.

Captain Steve Dutfield was a secondary school teacher for 13 years prior to becoming a Salvation Army officer. Having served in the Welsh valleys for five years as the leader of a local Salvation Army Corps with his wife Gillian, he now encourages prospective officers to explore the relationship between Faith and Culture, through teaching Mission and Platform Ministry at William Booth College, London. He also coordinates the work of distance learning students. He is currently studying for a Masters degree in Applied Theology at Moorlands College.

Rev Canon Anne Dyer is Warden of Cranmer Hall, St John's College, Durham. Cranmer Hall is an Anglican Theological College. Prior to taking up this post Anne was responsible for the continuing ministerial development of clergy, including curates, in the Diocese of Rochester.

Rob Frost was a Methodist minister and evangelist up until his death in 2007. Author, broadcaster and international speaker, his ministry founded Share Jesus missions, Easter People conferences and Seed Teams. Married to Jacqui with sons Andy and Chris, he was one of the most influential leaders of the church in the UK, especially in the area of growing young leaders.

Dr Peter Holmes has combined a career in management consultancy and service in Church and international mission. He holds an MA in pastoral psychology and a PhD in therapeutic faith community. His published works include *Becoming More Like Christ* and *Church As A Safe Place*. He is leader of Christ Church, Deal, Kent.

Derek Tidball was the principal of the London School of Theology (formerly LBC) for 12 years and has been on the staff of LST for a total of 26 years. A former President of the Baptist Union of Great Britain, he has also served as the pastor of two local churches and as Head of the BU's Mission Department. He is widely involved in the leadership of a number of Christian agencies and is a Vice-President of the Evangelical Alliance as well as a trustee and former chair of Network. Derek holds a PhD from Keele University and is a wide ranging author. He remains deeply involved in theological education and is a Visiting Scholar at Spurgeon's College.

Keith Warrington is Vice-Principal and Director of Doctoral Studies at Regents Theological College where he specializes in New Testament Studies, especially the role of the Spirit, healing and Pentecostal Theology.

Dr Susan B. Williams is a specialist in personal relational and organizational change and a qualified trainer. She is a management consultant with extensive experience in dramatics and therapeutic change. She is also director of several businesses and charities, and her remarkable personal journey is outlined in her autobiography *Letting God Heal*. She holds an MPhil and PhD in therapeutic change and her writings including *Changed Lives*, *Becoming More Like Christ* and *Church As A Safe Place*.

David Wilkinson is Principal of St John's College and Lecturer in the Department of Theology and Religion at Durham University. A Methodist minister, he is married to Alison and has two children. He specializes in the relationship of Christian faith to contemporary culture.

Heather Wraight's desire is to help Christian leaders, having been one herself for nine of her 22 years at Radio Worldwide, a ministry of WEC International. She was Deputy Director of Christian Research for 13 years, and editor of the *UK Christian Handbook*. Her qualitative research work provides insight into the issues Christians face in church life and elsewhere.

1

The Great Disconnection

Rev Dr Rob Frost

As co-editors of this book and friends of Rob Frost we are conscious that Rob finished his chapter only a few weeks before his death. This book comes out of Rob's passion and this chapter sums up his concerns and indeed remarkable achievements in enabling and equipping young people for ministry – a group of which we have both had the privilege to be part of.

David Wilkinson and Joanne Cox

Although I regularly teach in two theological colleges I don't consider myself to be an expert in theological education. First and foremost my ministry has been about evangelism, and about mentoring and equipping new Christians to stand firm and to grow in discipleship.

Over the 12 years that I led the 'Seed Team' gap year programme over 500 young people spent a year or more working on the frontline of mission with us. Since then, over 50 young people have worked for 12 months or more with my wife and I on the 'Vision Team'. I usually have at least two or three paid mentorees in their 20s in my core staff team who manage projects and who often travel with me; and currently there are eight young people on our new placement programme who come for periods of three to six months to live in community together and to work in mission alongside us.

My extensive experience of engaging in mission with young people in the 18–25 age group has meant that I am often with them during those years when they are exploring their vocation. Over the 20 years in which I have been immersed in this process I have become more and more disturbed about what happens when they begin to test a 'call to full-time ministry'. Sometimes recovering from the spiritual damage caused by this vocational journey has taken years. I have watched as some have 'tested a call' but found no opportunity in the Church to work through what they felt that God was calling them to do. Others have submitted themselves to following the traditional institutional pathway into ministry but, after years of 'going through the process' have found that the ministry on offer at the end of it was very limiting and not at all what they had thought they were 'signing up' to.

Thirty years ago, when I entered the Methodist ministry, the pathway to ordination was clear and there was no practical alternative. After sensing my 'call' I had to become a Methodist 'local preacher' (two years), then candidate for the Methodist ministry (one year), then attend theological college (four years), and then be placed on 'probation' (two years) before I could at last be 'ordained'. It was a laborious process even in the 1970s, and there were a number of times when I nearly quit (and a couple of occasions when I was nearly thrown out!).

Over the last 30 years this 'pathway' into the Methodist ministry has changed very little. Local preaching, candidature, and some form of theological education (either residential or by distance learning) is usually followed by a period of assessment during 'probation'. Systems in other denominations, although they have different names and processes, have also stayed much the same and generally follow the same pattern that they did 30 years ago. In the route to ordained ministry it seems that 'though the world may change about me … nothing changes here'.

My passion to instigate change through initiating this book, *The Call and the Commission*, is not driven by some aspiration to transform theological education or to challenge the institution to fresh expressions of ministry. No, it's primarily about the young people themselves. It's about the damage done to them when they can't find appropriate ways of following through the 'Call' that they have received. It's about the loss of Christian leadership because of it.

Those in national leadership on the Church scene need to take urgent and radical steps to ensure that we find the right kind of gifted leaders to serve the Church of the future. The present systems are failing us, and we need to design much more fluid ways of testing a call and equipping an emerging leader if we are to stem this haemorrhage of gifted talent.

Ultimately, this great 'disconnection' is the result of the limited forms of ministry the denominations are offering. God is still calling, but the Church is not providing the right opportunities to match this call. For this is not a call to a 'traditional' kind of church ministry but to different forms of leadership to serve the new demands of what the church is becoming. I fear that there's been a great disconnection between those whom God has been calling, and those whom the Church has been looking for!

This new call is a call to church planting and to a new style of contemporary 'missionary service' within the UK. It's often a call to a 'tent-making ministry' in which you follow your career whilst leading a church. It's a call to working with unchurched young people, or to working among those who are the most disadvantaged in society. It's a call to planting new kinds of churches, or to working with the established churches who are willing to think 'out of the box' in terms of their life and mission. It's a call to a kind of ministry which resonates with the highest traditions of Christian leadership, and which has little interest in 'status' or 'professional accreditation'. Ultimately it's a call to a radical kind of discipleship that is costly, visionary and non-institutional! The Church's failure to ratify this kind of call has resulted in a tragic haemorrhaging of new talent. God has been calling a new generation of Christian leaders to 'serve the present age' whilst the Church has been looking for leaders to serve an age long gone. It's this gap between the call received and the call the church is looking for which lies at the root of 'The Great Disconnection'.

I believe that this 'disconnection' is widening, with the result that some denominations have all but lost hope of recruiting significant numbers of young church leaders. Sadly, these cumbersome institutions sometimes seem to be more comfortable working with candidates in their mid-50s! This has resulted in an ageing church leadership profile nationally and has led to less and less effective missiological engagement. A new generation of radical and forward-thinking young people could have made such a difference! Whilst the Church has been looking for traditional 'ministers' to keep the local churches going, God has been calling a new generation of leaders to plant a new kind of Church altogether!

Over the centuries, the Church has been refreshed by each new generation of 'angry young men and women' emerging into Christian leadership. Where are they to be found in the Church today? Is it possible that God has actually been calling them, but that the Church has failed to embrace them or to affirm their call?

When I first began to discuss these concerns with the principals of several theological colleges I discovered that they had significant concerns too. On the one hand they are trying to recruit students in a very competitive 'market' and have to 'sell' courses which young students might actually want to study – most especially courses which pick up on this hunger to engage in new forms of ministry. On the other hand they are still expected to produce the kind of church leaders who are good 'all rounders' and who will fill denominational 'stations' or parishes. For while the traditional denominations hark on about 'fresh expressions' of church they don't seem able to provide the extensive financial resources to fund the ministers who will specialize in them!

These differing expectations are not the only problem which college principals face! The diminishing financial resources available from both the denominations and the government have made the 'bottom line' of running a college increasingly difficult. They are often forced to offer much more 'cost effective' distance learning options, and this leads to a sharp decrease in the 'contact time' which they can have with their students. All this comes at a time when there are ever higher academic expectations from the validating universities and an ever longer list of training expectations from the denominations.

If this collection of essays does nothing more than put these matters on the agenda of the contemporary church, then it won't have been in vain. I hope that the young people who are trying to interpret their 'call' will join this discussion and make their views heard. Above all, I hope that we'll all become a lot more sensitive to those young people who are 'testing a call', and a lot more serious about engaging with them about how that call might be played out in the life of the contemporary church.

I am not alone is my concerns about this. Lyle Schaller, writing in *Innovations in Ministry* concluded that

> From the perspective of the year 2018, perhaps the most far-reaching bad news is the inability of today's theological seminaries to attract adequate numbers of highly competent, exceptionally gifted, deeply committed, and clearly extroverted adults born after 1965 who possess a compelling call to the parish ministry ... The time has arrived for a new system of enlisting, training, screening, and credentialing the next generation of parish pastors.[1]

I will leave others who are more informed about theological education to explore what the great 'disconnection' means in their context. As for me, my contribution to this debate is to try and identify the issues that the young people themselves have been struggling with; issues which lie deep at the root of this 'great disconnection'. If this essay reads like something of a 'rant' it comes from my passion to protect the young people going through the process of exploring vocation – and my frustrations with denominational institutions over many years!

The call to evangelism

My own call to the ministry was very much part of my 'call to evangelism'. In my early 20s I discovered a passion to share the good news about Jesus, and a deep longing that others might know Him as I did. I soon discovered that the denomination in which I had found my faith was quite sceptical about such a call. To me, they seemed to view the 'presbyteral ministry' as much more about pastoral work, preaching, teaching, social engagement, and church management rather than evangelism. The gift of the 'evangelist' was certainly not seen as particularly crucial to any call to ministry. I remained convinced that God had called me to be an ordained evangelist, however, but in the long pathway of candidature I often felt that my main gift seemed the least appropriate, and that the most significant part of my call was the least affirmed.

As I have observed the journey which many young people have taken over the last 20 years it has often seemed reminiscent of my own. Many of them have come to a passionate faith in Christ, and have discovered His grace, healing and forgiveness for themselves. This good news has transformed their lives, and they are soon burning with a passion to share it with others. Their passion for the lost is integral to their call, so it's little wonder that they feel confused when it doesn't seem to be exactly what the Church is looking for.

This disconnection has undoubtedly been accentuated by the rising popularity of gap year mission projects over the last 20 years. The tens of thousands of young people have travelled to the furthest corners of the earth to share their faith with agencies like Operation Mobilization, Youth With a Mission, Oasis or Youth For Christ, which has given them a passion for mission and service which sees a great urgency in 'getting on with it' rather than talking about it.

When I was being interviewed for the ordained ministry nearly 40 years ago I was already working among some of the tough skinhead gangs of Deptford in Inner London. As I faced the various committees I felt that I was getting over the different hurdles put before me in spite of my call to evangelism rather than because of it! Lots of young people tell me that they have felt the same. I have actually found myself advising candidates for ministry to 'tone down' their passion for evangelism so that they might present themselves to interviewing panels in a rather more 'balanced' way.

It's very easy for those who grace such boards to view this passion for evangelism with suspicion. Such candidates are sometimes regarded as 'theologically naïve', 'unteachable' or 'too immature' for Christian ministry. They have sometimes been directed to work for para-church agencies and have received the signal that their call wasn't quite appropriate for the ordained ministry.

I'm convinced that in an age of rampant secularization and diminishing church attendance God has been calling a new generation of evangelists to lead His Church. I believe that the older mainline denominations have lost innumerable 'ministerial candidates' for ministry to the 'new' streams because of their inability to affirm the gift of the evangelist as integral to the ordained ministry.

Personally, I would be very suspicious of any young candidate offering for ministry without a passion for the lost! If they don't have it at 20, I dread to think what kind of vision would be left after 40 years of demanding ministry! Is it possible that in a time of great retrenchment that God's been sending the Church a new 'sales force' – a sales force that its leaders didn't even recognize they needed?

Such blindness hasn't always been prevalent in the mainline denominations. When the leaders at the 1744 Methodist Conference discussed the need for a seminary their primary concern was 'how can the preachers be made more effective evangelists?' When the first college began, some 90 years later, it was clear that the syllabus was designed to equip the students to do the 'work of an evangelist'. Theological education in many of Methodism's colleges continued with this kind of emphasis for generations.

W.E. Sangster, the great Methodist preacher, once reminisced about his college in Richmond,

> In the first years of the College's life the numerous references to the opening of new 'preaching rooms' and new chapels in the riverside area become almost monotonous. All the villages in the neighbourhood (Richmond was still rural then) were visited from house to house: conversation on the step and prayer in the home was the common strategy, and a tract was left as a souvenir of the call.

Sangster concluded, 'The anxiety to get people saved runs like a golden thread through all the record of a hundred years'.[2]

How things have changed! I will never forget the phone call I made to the ministerial training office of my own denomination several years ago. The young man in my front room had four top-grade A levels, had been a member of our Seed Team for two years. He was so outstanding that we made him a leader at 19. He told me about his call to the ordained ministry. 'But two things matter to me, the first is that I'm an evangelist, and secondly that I want to give my life to planting churches.'

I dialled the number and repeated his story to the refined gentleman at ministerial training. He replied, 'Well, er, he doesn't sound the sort of chap for us. Has he tried the Baptists?' Thankfully, the Anglicans took him on that basis, and he is now exercising a stunning ministry in one of the most difficult overseas locations that I know.

As I have worked with scores of young evangelists throughout my ministry I have seen in many of them the potential for outstanding leadership. Sadly the denominations have somehow communicated that the gift of the evangelist is not exactly what they were looking for. I'm convinced that there's been a great disconnection between those whom God has been calling, and those whom the Church has been trying to recruit.

I must add an important rider to this, however. In no way do I wish to devalue the call to pastoral ministry, or to more traditional forms of church leadership. God is still calling young women and men to this role, and their gifts are still desperately needed. I fear, sadly, that the role of the evangelist and the church planter has been much devalued throughout my ministry, and the Church is now paying heavily for its lack of respect for these important aspects of Christian ministry.

The call to the here and now

I first began to explore the possibility of full-time Christian service when I was just 20 years of age, but I was shocked to discover what a cumbersome process it was. The prospect of seven long years of preparation when I was 20 felt like a lifetime. I only got through it by organizing large-scale missions throughout my training (often to the amusement and concern of my tutors!).

This kind of impatience with the institutional process is very evident among many of the young people I work with today. There is a deep frustration with the Church, and a real suspicion about its institutional culture. Many of these young leaders feel that the spiritual state of the nation is too critical to spend time playing denominational games.

When one of the dynamic young evangelists working with me senses a call to full-time Christian service they don't want to spend seven years 'in training' before they begin. They want to start next month, and preferably sooner! In this special 'season' in which their call comes loud and clear they often make a response which is total and immediate. The urgency of the call means that they want to 'get going', to 'reach the world' and to invest their energy in the 'here and now' of God's Kingdom.

The Church fails to recognize the immediacy of this call and can't seem to understand that this is how God works today and that this is how today's generation responds. Just as Isaiah responded with the words 'Here I am, send me!' those receiving the call don't want to reply 'Here I am, please send me on a seven-year assessment programme to check that I'm not making it up!'

The Holy Spirit often works in 'Kairos moments' of Call and Response. Again and again the Church has 'blown the moment of opportunity' by showering the bright-eyed new 'candidate' with a torrent of paperwork, examinations, tests, interviews, courses, and assessments. It's little wonder that this process sometimes seems as if it's actually obstructing the call rather than facilitating it! The process seems to be primarily about serving the needs of the 'institution' rather than responding to the needs of the one hearing a 'call'.

Some young people have been told 'Come back in ten or twenty years' time, when you've had more experience of the world and proven yourself in some other field'. What absolute poppycock! If such criteria had been applied to most of the great 'calls' in the Bible we'd only be left with feisty geriatrics like Abraham, Sarah and Methuselah as our primary models of obedience!

The church needs leaders in their early 20s, and if I had my way I'd take them at 18! Some of our most effective years in ministry can be in our 20s, and if we don't release people into leadership then, how can we possibly grow the next generation of senior Christian leaders? The Church will always need spiritual giants who have given a whole lifetime to Christian service, mission and training. Where will they come from if most folk only really start in ministry at 50?

The Church puts up too many hurdles and takes the role of interrogator rather than facilitator. The Church seems to stick with a Victorian 'are you good enough?' style of recruitment rather than trying to engage with the possibilities of what each new candidate might be able to bring! Some of the processes smack of a kind of conservatism among older ministers which whispers 'I went through it, so why shouldn't they?' It's little wonder that new candidates start to 'cool off', question whether they had a call at all, or start seeking out agencies who are prepared to 'let them loose' much more quickly and with a much lighter touch.

Part of the historic baggage which many church denominations carry is their regard for Christian Ministry as a 'profession' like that of a lawyer, doctor or accountant. To preserve this status the Church has added standards of accreditation which some young people can never hope to aspire to. We need to re-visit such outdated assumptions and unbiblical expectations.

We are in an era in which church leaders may be persecuted and we're coming to a time when the true measure of a Christian leader will be about wisdom, spiritual gifts and integrity. Academic prowess or an ability to flourish in a middle class professional setting will not feature large in such an anti-Christian culture! Alan Roxburgh observes that 'The seminary has assumed a social function within the canons of modernity ... The symbols of the pedagogue and the professional belong to a period when the pastor did function at the cultural centre'.[3]

In the UK that age is long gone. We need to train people to re-evangelize the nation, not to become 'pillars' of its middle class society. Some of the rough and ready evangelists who I have mentored during the course of my ministry could never jump through the academic hoops which the denominations set before them. Most church panels won't even consider candidates if they don't have a bunch of decent A levels! Some of my most effective mission leaders never stood a chance in such an environment! To get them educationally 'up to speed' would have taken a lifetime, and many of them were just too educationally disadvantaged to give it a go.

The most pressing need is for courses which actually recognize that some candidates have very limited educational achievements. Many more have scarce biblical knowledge, a scant understanding of personal spirituality, a lack of experience of effective evangelism and a very limited idea of what it means to take up the towel of humble Christian service. The most urgent priority is to bring candidates 'up to speed' with the most basic grounding in Christian teaching.

Some of these natural-born leaders come from social contexts which are a world away from the ivory towers of theological colleges. Uprooting them would take them out of the very place where they can flourish, and moving them into an academic context is just a leap too far.

The film *Educating Rita* lifted the main character out of her social milieu so that she was no longer able to relate to those around her. In the same way the Church has sometimes tried to take gifted evangelists out of their natural culture only to destroy their effectiveness to reach the people from which they came! Theological education needs to be taken to them and made relevant to their context. Training for ministry is not about lifting people into a middle class social status, but about equipping them to lead the people of God where they are. God calls seemingly 'educationally challenged' leaders and I don't believe that they need to spend years in an 'ivory tower' to be great in the Kingdom of God! As Steve Chalke once observed

> ... I never cease to be surprised and, at the same time, relieved by the limited understanding of the disciples – they constantly seem to miss the point of what Jesus is saying and doing. They have an inexhaustible capacity to get hold of the wrong end of the stick ... The disciples, it is fair to say, were far from perfect. Yet it is to this rough band of working men that Jesus chose to entrust his continuing mission. Let us be in no doubt: God is happy to work with sinners.[4]

Many churches also assume that a call is automatically for life. A young person responding to a call at 20 is regarded as 'signing on' for a minimum term of 45 years – a term of office which even the Army, Navy or Air Force do not require! It's unfair that a retired accountant at 55 who has 'a call' is welcomed to sign up for church leadership for the remaining five or 10 years of their active working life. A 20-year-old is expected to do the full term!

The young people I work with are as committed to the call they receive as ever, and they are completely 'sold out' for Jesus. Many of them do see it as 'for life', but they are unsure as to exactly what 'shape' this Christian service will take over the next 40 years. They have no idea what kind of people they will become in 30 years' time, and have no desire to shut down their options at such a young age.

Most of their peers will have at least three careers in a lifetime, so it seems unfair to them that the Church of God so tightly defines what they will do for the rest of their lives. The young people I work with say 'I'm ready to answer God's call now and it's a call for life … but ask me in ten years time if it will still be the parish ministry!' In inviting young people to follow a call into full-time Christian leadership it should be made clear that this call might take a diverse range of expressions over a lifetime. As I look at many of my 'peers' in theological college, it's clear that over the 30 years since we had our 'valedictory,' that few of us have actually remained exclusively in the 'parish ministry' throughout that lifetime of service.

Our vocation has been a 'live' and unfolding journey throughout the many chapters of our lives. The older I get, the more convinced I am that God works with us just like this. We don't get a 'lifetime package' defining our ministry at the moment of 'call'; but when we respond we commit ourselves to spending a lifetime working out what the call actually means in our ongoing personal journey.

This is the 'here and now' generation: the planet might burn up, the Church go bankrupt or the Christians be locked up long before they reach retirement! This call is too urgent for them to think of it as an unchanging 'job description' covering the next 40 years! One young man used to come to our student meetings in a local college and heckle. He was an outspoken atheist and gave our student mission team a real run-around, but eventually he found Christ. He was desperate to serve God in the here and now. I remember discussing with him how my denomination would be asking him for seven years of training and accreditation and 40 years of unstinting parish 'service', and I can still see the look on his face.

The local Pentecostal church asked him to plant a new congre-gation on one of the toughest estates in south-west London. He made no commitment to a lifetime of Christian service, yet they still mentored him, sent him away for short periods of training, helped him to study for a higher degree, and gradually integrated him into the leadership of the mother church. He is now the senior pastor of that large church, has an outstanding preaching ministry, and is moving his growing congregation to a massive new facility so that they can all get in.

The leaders of that Pentecostal church understood the urgency of his call, his passion for the here and now and his frustration with institutional Christianity. They also knew the value of mentorship, action-reflection, further theological training, and higher degrees. If you compared his qualifications at this point in his ministry with someone trained in a traditional 'start up' college education I think you'd have to admit that he is just as well equipped, if not more so. His training has been 'on the job', directly applied to his needs, and enriched with a mix of local and national input. Above all, his 'Kairos' moment was not lost in institutional process, and he was never asked to sign up for life! The elders of that church moved him into Christian leadership when they were sure that his call was genuine and then tailor-made the training to fit his needs rather than putting him through some kind of ministerial production line.

This system isn't without its dangers, however. In *ChurchNext* by Ian Coffey and Eddie Gibbs the authors warn that

> … many newer churches are growing their own church leaders from within and training them on the job. For all the strengths of the approach, however (and it has real strengths), this pattern has some weaknesses and may not persist in the longer term. Such training can be dangerously close to cloning rather than to education. It does not allow for the systematic and rapid growth in understanding which more traditional courses offer. And, as yet, it does not lead to the transferable and recognized qualification which the wider world considers so important.[5]

One of the challenges to theological educators today is how to engage with the serious dangers and weaknesses which on-the-job training can seed. They urgently need to devise courses which will work among those training *in situ* among the people with whom they feel comfortable. Another is to develop ongoing training schemes which will offer support to those who will be the mentors and local educators of these emerging leaders.

Theological educators must sit down with those who are leading the newer churches to try and discover how theological education fits into this developmental process. The institutional managers responsible for 'ministerial recruitment and training' must learn from these newer models and emulate what is working well in other contexts.

My greatest fear is that localized forms of training and 'distance learning' can lead to a 'dumbing down' of theological education. The Church of the future will still need Hebrew scholars, theologians, missiologists, and leaders with the kind of broad-based theological education that gives them a wisdom and maturity which will equip them for national and international Christian leadership. Heaven forbid that localized training, distance learning or on-the-job education will completely replace the residential college environment. There must always be space for outstanding young scholars to be supported in devoting quality time to thought and study.

An outstanding young Bible scholar, with an ability to hold over 2,000 people in rapt attention for an hour when he spoke at Easter People, asked me how he could be equipped for a lifetime of scholarship and teaching of the biblical texts. His science First from Oxford made him a very able candidate. We contacted a number of major colleges asking how this young man could be supported in doing a theology degree and then a biblical Studies PhD. I drew a blank. Somehow he didn't fit the criteria that anyone was looking for. He is not the only outstanding young scholar who I've seen slip through the fingers of the Church. It's little short of a tragedy.

The focus needs to move from 'how can the church train the ministers it needs?' to 'how can the church train the leaders who God sends?' There needs to be a far greater flexibility of training options from *in situ* to on the job, and from 'specialist academic' to 'basic Christian teaching'. Above all, we need to seize the moment when the call is heard, and empower people to start in a mentored setting of ministry before having to jump through hundreds of professional hoops in order to be considered.

Managers or leaders?

Over the last 10 years it's been my privilege to be a member of the Faculty of the International Leadership Institute which is based in Atlanta. My work with them has taken me to many parts of the world, and given me the opportunity to share in leadership conferences with outstanding Christian leaders from many nations.

Sadly, I find the same story repeated again and again all over the world. Christian leaders, some of them carrying enormous national and international responsibilities, tell me that 'no one taught me about leadership'. Even the basic fundamentals about vision, mobilization, leadership integrity and the skills involved in mentoring our successors have never been learnt. These leaders have been left to figure out what leadership is and have often struggled in the process.

The young people who I mix with are invariably sensing a call to Christian leadership. They don't see themselves as called to middle management in some brand of institutional Christianity that is withering on the vine. They will not devote their lives to some wishy-washy style of leadership which asks no one to follow! Yet the image of contemporary Christian leadership often looks just like this. They fear that even after seven years of appraisal and training, they will be so encumbered with 'managerial' responsibilities in the local church, that they'll have precious little time or energy left to make a difference.

We need a massive re-education of the faithful around the country; the leaders of tomorrow must not be people pleasers, time servers or church bureaucrats. Their primary agenda must be mission, and they will need to be the kind of people who can carry a vision, mobilize the Church and think with a blue-sky agenda! If they aren't like this, there will be no church left for them to serve anyway. The world is changing, and we're going to need new kinds of leaders who are able to make massive leaps in imaginative mission if they are to reach such an alienated society.

J.P. Kolter of the Harvard Business School makes a clear distinction between leadership and management. Leadership has vision, communicates vision, and has the ability to get others to follow. Such leaders can recruit and motivate people to work to the vision by inspiring and directing them. This is different from the management function which ensure an efficient use of resources.

Managers administer; leaders innovate. Managers are systems focused; leaders are people focused. Managers rely on control;

leaders rely on trust. Managers must watch the bottom line; leaders must watch the horizon. The best leaders combine a concern for details with a grasp of the big picture. They have moved beyond the command and control model of leading to a more flexible, empowering, energizing style that makes people feel valued and liberated to take risks.

The young people who I see emerging on the Christian scene have a clear vision about what God is calling them to do, and a willingness to sacrifice everything to get the job done! Deep down they know that they are being called to lead, not to manage. They are ready to call others to follow, and they don't want to hang around waiting for a consensus. They believe passionately in the empowerment of others, and in the healthy function of the body of Christ but ultimately the call on their lives is to lead.

In many contexts the traditional denominations seem to have failed to bring young people into authentic leadership at a young enough age. There seems to have been an unwillingness to empower them, and because we have waited too long to do so, they have gone elsewhere where their gifts seemed more welcome and the opportunities to lead seemed more real. We have preferred to weigh them down with examinations and appraisals rather than setting them free to have a go themselves, with proper systems of support and accountability.

At one of our Easter People events no one was allowed to have a 'platform role' without someone under 25 shadowing them and sharing the ministry. Often the younger set of leaders had more to bring than any of us had dared to hope for. I have watched as some of them have gone through the production line of candidature, training and oversight ... and seen this 'leadership' passion being gently but firmly squeezed out. When they do emerge to work in some local context they have lost the confidence to see through what needs to be done! I'm convinced that God is calling forward a new generation of servant leaders who are not middle managers. Many of these new leaders have a great entrepreneurial flair, which, if given free reign, will open boundless new opportunities for local Christian mission and service.

Sadly, the Church rarely recognizes this kind of gifting. We prefer to lumber young firebrands with twelve country chapels and no one alongside to give them permission to 'dream a new dream'! It's little wonder that their contemporaries are reticent to follow in their footsteps! Having endured years of assessment and accreditation they feel 'conned' because the Church has given them a job where they'll never have time to get beyond maintenance and into mission!

Many of the congregations who they serve have expectations which are simply unrealistic. They still see the 'minister' in the traditional role as one who 'serves the faithful' and who just doesn't have time to engage with the world. It's little wonder that young people don't want to subject themselves to such models of ministry which seem more reminiscent of 'More tea, vicar?' than prophetic engagement with a hurting and broken world.

There is a desperate need in the Church for strong, God-anointed, Christ-centred leaders. There is too much ego, too much pride and too much 'self sufficiency' in today's models of church leadership, and it's little wonder that young people are questioning whether it's truly biblical, and whether they want any part in it. The contemporary scene demands that Christian leaders should be visionary and expert at networking.

> Networking leaders are not jealous of one another's positions. Instead, they recognise the gifts of those around them. They do not feel threatened or 'upstaged' by persons with greater expertise in areas vital to the success of a project. They are ambitious for the people around them. They encourage new teams to spin off to develop alternative approaches to the same problems or to tackle new issues. Networking leaders see structures in terms of organic interconnectedness and not as an inflexible, mechanistic framework.[6]

Over the years, I have watched in horror as leaders like this – leaders who have already proven their immense capacity to lead in frontline mission situations – are rejected by the denominational church. In my view, the three most outstanding leaders who God gave the Church in the UK in the last 20 years are now all making a very good living 'in the world'. The Church didn't recognize what they had to offer, use them in appropriate contexts, or give them sufficient freedom to flourish.

Theological education must engage with this call to leadership, and give those called resources to function effectively as leaders. We must all ensure that the Church uses these remarkable people in the kind of contexts where their gifts are best used.

Connecting with the call and the commission

If the Church of today wants to release the right leaders into the Church of tomorrow it needs to be on the look-out for young people with a heart and passion for evangelism. It needs to listen to what they are saying about their call, rather than trying to make them fit the models of a previous age. The Church needs to find ways of releasing them into front-line Christian service quickly, while covering the bases of induction, training and mentorship as they travel fast on the journey to becoming leaders.

The Church shouldn't talk about lifetime commitments, or 40-year pension plans. This is the 'here and now' generation, and they don't want to become 'professional parsons' – they want to discover a context where they can flourish and mature as Christian leaders now. A place where there's support, mentorship and trust. We don't need to remove them all from the cultural context in which they thrive to join the ministry – we can train them where they live if that's what they need! But they will need training appropriate to their individual educational levels.

If Starbucks claims to be the happiest place to work in the UK, it's laying down a challenge to the Christian Church to become an even happier, more fulfilling, exciting, rewarding, and stimulating place to be. For we're not just baristas, we're family; and we're not just serving up frothy coffee – we're offering the Water of Life itself!

Bibliography

Chalke, Steve, with Anthony Watkins, *Intelligent Church* (Grand Rapids, MI: Zondervan, 2006).

Coffey, Ian and Eddie Gibbs, *ChurchNext* (Leicester: InterVarsity Press, 2001).

Roxburgh, Alan, *The Missionary Congregation: Leadership and Liminality* (Philadelphia, PA: Trinity Press International, 1997).

Sangster, W., 'Richmond College' in Frank H. Cumbers (ed.), *Richmond College 1843–1943* (Peterborough: Epworth, 1944).

Schaller, Lyle, *Innovations in Ministry* (Nashville, TN: Abingdon, 1994).

Notes

1. Schaller, Lyle, *Innovations in Ministry* (Nashville, TN: Abingdon, 1994).
2. Sangster, W.E., 'Richmond College' in Frank H. Cumbers (ed.), *Richmond College 1843–1943* (Peterborough: Epworth, 1944).
3. Roxburgh, Alan, *The Missionary Congregation: Leadership and Liminality* (Philadelphia, PA: Trinity Press International, 1997), 17.
4. Chalke, Steve, with Anthony Watkins, *Intelligent Church* (Grand Rapids, MI: Zondervan, 2006).
5. Coffey, Ian and Eddie Gibbs, *ChurchNext* (Leicester: InterVarsity Press, 2001).
6. Coffey and Gibbs, *ChurchNext*.

2

Called According to His Purpose

Dr Peter Brierley and Heather Wraight

The familiar words of Romans 8:28 – 'We know that all things work together for good to them who are the called according to His purpose' – have been of wide comfort to those caught in difficult situations in the normal affairs of life. They refer to all believers not just ministers, as does Paul's general encouragement to live a holy life in Ephesians 4:1 'lead a life worthy of the calling with which you were called.'[1] However, the Authorized Version of this latter verse is 'walk worthy of the vocation …' and as so many ministers think of their work as their *vocation*, this chapter considers just how many ministers or clergy have taken up this particular sacred vocation in the UK.

The publication *Religious Trends*[2] gives a total of 35,400 ministers in the UK in 2006, a number which is only slightly larger than the 35,300 in 2000, although the slight increase is expected to grow over the next few years. While the actual numbers have not changed much, we shall see that how they are made up has varied. However, these totals immediately beg at least two questions – how do they compare with other professions, and how do they match other statistics about the Church? The first question is answered as follows with the percentage being the increase or decrease during the 1990s:[3]

Engineers (chartered)	194,000	–	3%
Accountants (chartered)	132,000	+	31%
Doctors	121,000	+	38%
Solicitors (practising)	80,000	+	40%
Surveyors (chartered)	83,000	+	46%
Estate agents	45,000	+	41%

Secretaries (chartered)	44,000	+ 183%
Pharmacists	44,000	+ 256%
Ministers of religion	35,000	– 3%
Dentists	32,000	+ 67%
Architects	30,000	+ 7%

Ministers of religion and engineers are the only two of the 11 largest professions in the country which have lost numbers. All the others have increased, some significantly.

With respect to the second question, the increase of 100 in the number of ministers in the years 2000 to 2006 (+ 0.004%), compares remarkably closely with the change in the number of churches, 48,400, in 2006 which was just 400 fewer than in 2000 (–0.008%). Numbers of buildings and numbers of leaders may remain stationary, but this is in marked contrast to the people of God whose membership of the churches decreased from 6.0 million in 2000 to 5.7 million by 2006 (a drop of –5%), while attendance declined from 4.4 million in the year 2000 to 3.8 million in Great Britain in 2006 (a decline of –14%).[4]

So the number of ministers in total does not change, unlike their flock, but what other characteristics do they have?

Numbers by country

The number of ministers in the four constituent countries of the UK are shown in Table 1, where the last column refers to the 2006 figures.

Table 1   Number of clergy in 2000 and 2006 by country

Country	2000	2006	% change	2006 as % of total
England	28,400	28,600	+1%	81
Wales	1,800	1,800	0	5
Scotland	3,300	3,200	–5%	9
N Ireland	1,800	1,800	0	5
TOTAL	35,300	35,400	+ ½%	100

The gains in England are slightly offset by losses in Scotland, but these movements are of insignificant of themselves. We need to dig a little deeper.

Numbers by denomination

Table 2 breaks down the number of ministers by the 10 major groups into which the 275 denominations of the UK are organized.[5]

Table 2   Number of clergy in 2000 and 2006 by denomination

Denomination	2000	2006	% change	2006 as % of total
Anglican	10,800	9,900	–9%	28
Baptist	2,700	3,000	+11%	8
R Catholic	6,900	6,100	–11%	17
Independent	1,800	2,000	+8%	6
Methodist	2,400	2,200	–9%	6
New Churches	2,300	2,700	+18%	8
Orthodox	300	300	0	1
Pentecostal	3,300	4,800	+44%	13
Presbyterian	2,700	2,400	–8%	7
Smaller denoms.	2,100	2,000	–2%	6
TOTAL	35,300	35,400	+ ½%	100%

The reasons why these numbers are changing varies. There are a larger number of Anglican full-time stipendiary priests retiring in the early twenty-first century than might normally be expected. This is because there was an especial influx of clergy 40 years ago, partly as a result of the number of young men converted at the Billy Graham Haringey Crusade in 1954, who are reaching retirement.

The Roman Catholics are generally failing to attract young men into the priesthood, a problem that has existed for at least a decade, and is not limited to the UK. It is assumed this is partly because of several abuse scandals in the UK and elsewhere and partly because priests may not marry (one survey showed 91 per cent of priests thought they could be married and still be a valid priest[6]). As a result existing priests are being asked to continue serving well into their 70s.

The New Churches, especially Newfrontiers, are continuing to plant more churches, which require new leaders. The Pentecostals are doing the same, but many of their new congregations are black congregations which often have several part-time ministers rather than one or two full-time ministers. The numbers include therefore some part-time ministers.

The Methodist and United Reformed Church, which is in the Presbyterian group in Table 2 because of its origins, are both closing churches. Does the loss of leaders follow the closure of churches, or vice versa? Whichever, the number of leaders has declined in tandem.

Age of ministers

This leads on to looking at the age of ministers, which is shown in Table 3. The information comes from the 2005 English Church Census, as the relevant question has not been asked in other countries. However, England has four-fifths, 81 per cent, of all the ministers in the UK (Table 1).

Table 3 shows the high percentage of Roman Catholic, Independent and Orthodox ministers or priests who are 70 or over. This is a serious problem for these churches, but others also face problems. Based on normal mortality applied to the total percentages above, some 11 per cent of current serving ministers will die in the next 10 years. That means across the board recruiting 400 ministers per year just to replace deaths in service, let alone retirements.

Denominational leaders are concerned and many are seeking to take appropriate action to ensure they have sufficient man- or woman-power for their needs. The Anglican Church especially

Denomination	Under 40 %	40 to 49 %	50 to 59 %	60 to 69 %	70 and over %	Average age	Base (=100%)
Anglican	6	24	44	25	1	54	2,862
Baptist	14	25	36	20	5	53	750
R Catholic	5	14	30	36	15	59	1,448
Independent	8	22	30	25	15	57	269
Methodist	9	26	40	21	4	53	613
New Churches	15	29	38	13	5	51	683
Orthodox	0	14	21	41	24	63	87
Pentecostal	8	30	32	21	9	54	1,221
Presbyterian	7	23	39	27	4	55	192
Smaller denoms.	11	24	38	19	8	54	537
TOTAL	8	24	37	24	7	54	8,662

has been very active in ordaining more people as Non-stipendiary Ministers (NSMs) or Ordained Local Ministers (OLMs) as well as encouraging older people, in their 50s for example, to seek ordination training. Figure 1 below shows the proportion by different age-groups of Church of England ministers in training over the 10 years 1994 to 2005.

It is clear that there has been a large increase in older people being recommended for training for Church of England ministry; those aged 50 or over were 14 per cent of the total in 1994 but had increased to over a third, 34 per cent, by 2005. This has several implications. On the positive side there is a growing number of mature trainees with considerable experience of life and work which can be of great benefit to a church.

Figure 1 Those recommended for ordination training, 1994–2005, by age

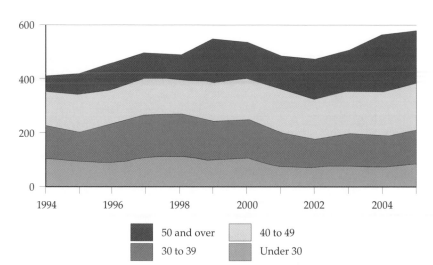

On the other hand, older trainees will have fewer years of service to offer once they are ordained, meaning few are likely to gain sufficient church experience to be considered for senior leadership positions such as Bishops and Archdeacons. It also means the proportional cost of each trainee per year they serve is higher. In addition, many 'family-friendly' churches would like a minister with a young family but older ministers, if married, are likely to have seen their family grow up. Ministers are most likely to attract people within 10 years of their own age so if a growing number of new ministers are aged over 50 who is going to be able to attract those aged under 40, the adult age group already least well represented in church?

Gender of ministers

Women ministers have received quite a lot of attention in recent years for a variety of reasons. By 2006, 15 per cent of ministers were female, a percentage which has been steadily rising ever since women were ordained in the Church of England in 1994 and

Figure 2   Number of male and female ministers, UK, all denominations, 1992–2010

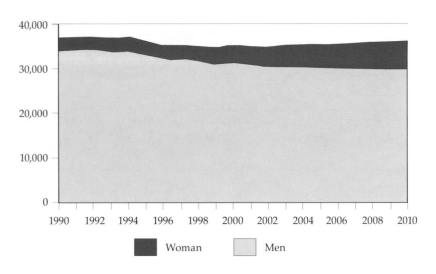

Woman   Men

which will almost certainly continue to increase. However, it is not just that the percentage of female ministers is increasing, the actual number is increasing at a time when the number of male ministers is decreasing. Figure 2 shows the number of ministers in the UK since gender was first counted across all denominations in 1992 and indicates that the proportion of female ministers is increasing as well as their number.[7]

The Salvation Army, who have appointed women as officers equally with men right from their inception, had the highest percentage of female ministers in 2006 – 54 per cent, but other denominations with significant percentages included the United Reformed Church with 42 per cent, the Methodists with 32 per cent, the Church of Scotland with 19 per cent and the Church of England with 18 per cent. In contrast, the Roman Catholic and Orthodox churches do not have any female priests at all, along with some other smaller denominations or groups.

According to the 2005 English Church Census, the largest church which had a female minister was a Church of England parish in North Yorkshire with a total Sunday attendance of 297.

The 6 per cent of churches larger than that all had male ministers. Smaller churches, many of which are in rural areas, were more likely to have a female minister, so that while a male minister had an average congregation of 84, the average congregation with a female minister was less than half that: 37 people.

Female ministers were more likely to serve in rural churches, especially remoter rural churches where 16 per cent had a female minister. Only 7 per cent of city centre churches had a female minister, separate towns 9 per cent, though council estates had 11 per cent. One of the greatest differences between the gender of ministers was, however, in churchmanship.

Churchmanship of ministers

Churchmanship, or ethos as it is sometimes called, is a term used for belief systems. Churchgoers tend to describe themselves as High, Middle-of-the-Road or Low. Ministers use a more detailed description with words like Anglo-Catholic, Liberal, Broad, Evangelical and Charismatic. Many denominations have a correlation with one or more of these. Thus, Baptists, Independents, the smaller denominations are largely Evangelical;[8] New Churches and Pentecostals are largely Evangelical or Charismatic Evangelical; Methodists and the United Reformed Church have a majority who are Broad or Liberal (as well as Low Church for the Methodists); the Roman Catholics are largely Catholic. The Orthodox are not any of these, and, because they are small in number, are usually put in the 'Other' category instead of a special 'Orthodox' category just for them. The one denomination which spans several churchmanships is the Anglican, which in 2005 was split between Evangelical (34%), Broad/Liberal (29%), Anglo-Catholic/Catholic (23%) and Low Church/Others (14%).[9]

However, churchgoers' and ministers' churchmanships are not identical, as Table 4 makes clear. Some ministers ticked 'other' and gave various descriptions, either instead of or in addition to ticking a box. These descriptions have been assigned to categories where appropriate and the adjusted percentages are shown in the shaded columns in Table 4.[10]

The Call and the Commission

Table 4   Churchmanship of churchgoers and ministers

Churchmanship	Scottish church-goers, 2002[11] %	English church-goers, 2005[12] %	English male ministers, 2005[13] %		English female ministers, 2005 %	
			RT	Adjusted	RT	Adjusted
Anglo-Catholic	–	5	5	5	3	4
Broad	11	9	20	27	15	25
Catholic	32	27	9	10	4	6
Broad Evangelical	–	6	11	11	7	7
Mainstream Evangelical	14	18	6	8	4	6
Charismatic Evangelical	5	16	4	4	2	2
Reformed Evangelical	10	–	–		–	
Reformed	15	–	–		–	
Liberal	9	9	23	25	35	38
Low Church	4	7	5	9	6	11
Others	–	3	17	1	24	1
Base (= 100%)	570,130	3,166,200	7,593		1,069	

While Table 4 shows there are far fewer Charismatic Evangelicals in Scotland than England, it also shows the differences between the churchmanship of ministers and English churchgoers are very substantial. There are more ministers who are Broad or Liberal (a majority of the total if these two groups are combined) and far fewer who are Catholic, Mainstream or Charismatic Evangelical. There are also fewer female ministers who are Catholic or Evangelical and many more who are Liberal.

Part of the reason for the differences is that most Evangelical churches are larger than non-Evangelical churches (so therefore have more churchgoers). Also there are very many small churches, especially in the rural areas, often describing themselves as Broad, which may be the only church in the village and therefore usually seek to cater for anyone who comes.

The beliefs of ministers

The 2005 English Church Census was not the first time that the difference in churchmanship of church leaders and laity had been noted. An earlier study, *The Mind of Anglicans*, found the same in 2002, but looked further at the difference in the actual beliefs that the various groups held, as Table 5 shows.[14]

Table 5   Believing 'without question', Church of England, 2002

Statement	Church-goers %	Male ministers %	Female ministers %
I believe that Jesus Christ died to take away the sins of the world	75	76	65
I believe in God the Father who created the world	73	83	74
I believe that God the Father, Jesus Christ and the Holy Spirit are all equally God	67	78	70
I believe that the Holy Spirit is a person who empowers Christians today	63	77	74
I believe that Jesus Christ physically rose from the dead	61	68	53
I believe that faith in Jesus Christ is the only way by which we can be saved	61	53	39
I believe that Jesus Christ was born of a Virgin	n/a	58	33
Base (= 100%)	1,910	1,549	192

While ministers generally score higher than lay people in their beliefs in basic Christian tenets, the greater proportion of Evangelical churchgoers is reflected in the higher score about faith in Jesus Christ as the only way of salvation. The differences between male and female ministers are larger, however, in some respects, especially with the three statements at the bottom of the Table – belief in the resurrection, the uniqueness of Christ and the virgin birth. In all of these, female ministerial belief is much lower than that of male ministers and many churchgoers.

What type of person becomes a minister?

Meredith Belbin was a management consultant in Australia and at the Henley College of Management for a number of years in the 1970s, where he made his far-reaching observations on the nature of management teams. His key observation was that those working in team situations bring at least one of eight key skills to that task. Many may bring more than one. Very few bring six or seven or all eight. He further observed that not all the various combinations of these characteristics actually produce successful teams. There are some combinations which simply don't work.

The basic book in which his ideas are set out is *Management Teams*.[15] He produced a questionnaire which helped to identify which of these characteristics people have. It has been found to be remarkably robust and consistent over time, age, and both genders, as well as in different cultures and ethnic groups. By answering the questions on the Belbin sheet the different characteristics can be ascertained for a particular individual. Groups of ministers and churchgoers have from time to time completed these forms, and Table 6 summarizes the results of some of the relevant surveys. It should be noted that only the top skill for each person is included, not all the skills they may have.

Table 6 shows that the type of team skill most common among ministers is that of Resource people – those who frequently know where to find something, know where to go to get a certain skill, or know people who do. They are excellent at networking and highly useful in situations where many different types of need may be present, as is true in most churches.

Table 6 Team leadership characteristics of ministers and lay people

Team type	Anglican ministers, Bradford Diocese, 1995[16] %	Christian Research members, 1997[17]			Ministers, all denominations, 2002[18] %	Overall weighted answers of ministers %[19]
		Anglican ministers %	Non-Anglican ministers %	Lay people %		
A Creative person	11	8	3	9	7	7
B Critic	13	14	10	8	10	10
C Detail person	18	3	13	9	7	8
D Resource person	15	26	21	19	20	20
E Task worker	7	7	14	17	11	11
F People worker	17	7	13	9	13	13
G Director leader	8	18	13	14	18	17
H Shaper leader	10	17	13	15	14	14
Base (= 100%)	42	90	77	138	1,002	1,211

A third of ministers, 31 per cent (types G and H together), are natural leaders, though these two types are different. The Leadership type G is the Director or Co-ordinator type and H the Shaper type. The Shaper is a driver who often tends to make things happen either by the force of his or her personality or because of the relevance of circumstances. The Shaper operates on the principle 'Why?' – what is the reason for this particular action, what is its purpose, what do we hope to achieve by doing this? The Director operates on the basis of 'How?' and seeks to indicate the ways by which actions can be fulfilled, how a vision can be worked out, the mechanisms that need to be in place in order to ensure that something happens. Often, but not always, the Director is better with people than a Shaper. It is these two which when present on a team can bring intolerable strain on relationships because of their different ways of leading, and some teams break under that strain.

The smallest percentage of ministers are Creative people, those who think of radical solutions to problems and pastoral situations. Could it be that creativity is perhaps overlooked in the evaluation of potential ordinands?

While based on small numbers, it is interesting to note that the proportion of lay people who are Task people is much higher than for ministers – just as well, if the work of the Church is to get done!

The 2002 survey (column 5) was primarily about the factors which enabled churches to grow, and was sponsored by the Salvation Army. It showed one leadership type was critical for growth – those ministers who are Shapers are much more likely to be leading a growing church. They are very likely to have a clear vision of where they want to go and a strategy of how to get there, and this is frequently a winning combination for developing a larger congregation over time.

Personality Profile

Professor Leslie Francis of the University of Wales has in recent years researched the personality profiles of various groups of people, including ministers, but to date has only published results for Welsh Anglican ministers. His main findings may be summarized as:

> Male clergy are more introvert than extrovert, but not more so than the general population; Male clergy are more likely to be adjusted to the outer world than men generally; Male clergy tend to be more intuitive than most men, allowing the mind to inform the eye; but on the other hand Male clergy are twice as likely as men in the general population to be 'perceivers', making their 'decisions or judgements

on the basis of interpersonal and subjective appreciation of human values.[20]

What do ministers *do*?

Churches grow when the teaching is good, the welcome is warm, the atmosphere is friendly and the worship is relevant. Ministers are at the heart of all such activity; their personality in many ways becomes the culture of the church they are leading. David Wasdell headed up the Urban Church Project in the 1970s and through his research discovered that the average number of people a minister (or anyone else for that matter) can remember by name is about 150.[21]

This means that for a church to grow above 150–200 people, a second person is necessary, for the second person can help the communication process with the second 150 people; David stressed that the second has to be in place *before* the church has a realistic chance of growing. However, when a second person joins the leadership team, the dynamic of leadership and therefore the way they need to act changes, as the following list from one of Eddie Gibbs' early books make clear,[22] where the church sizes are adapted to English churches, and the '101–150' added:

Church size	Skill Level	Chief characteristic
Up to 50	Foreman	Able to be involved in any task
51 to 100	Supervisor	Responsible for people doing routine jobs
101 to 150	Junior management	Some delegation but no real accountability
151 to 350	Middle management	Delegation with accountability
351 to 750	Top management	Responsible for overall strategy and vision
Over 750	Chairman of the Board	Excites others with perception of what it will be like in five years' time, with free time to ensure he keeps in touch with grass-roots

Rev Philip Hacking was the vicar of Christ Church, a Church of England parish in Fulwood, Sheffield for many years in the latter half of the twentieth century. It grew to be one of the more significant churches in the country. One legendary story of his ministry is that one carol service a man called Will Smith came in, and was duly greeted by Philip who asked about his wife and family and said how welcome he was. Will didn't turn up again till five years later and as he walked in, Philip went up to him and said, 'Will, how nice to see you again! You haven't been for some while. Last time you came your wife was quite ill; is she better now? And how are your three children getting on?' Very few people can do that!

I met him once and asked him how he did it. He took me into a room in the church and showed me an index file of many hundreds of cards, each written on in his personal handwriting. They represented all, either individuals or households, who had ever come to Christ Church, including of course all the regular 1,000+ members. There was a marker sticking up vertically about half-way down. He pointed to it – 'that's where I've got to at the moment. Every day I come in here and pray for each of the people on these cards, one after the other, for an hour or so'. No growth comes easily, and mostly only after sacrificial prayer, a dedicated team effort, and earnest commitment to (and with) the leader's shared vision.

Welcoming new people and praying for visitors and church members may be an important part of what ministers do, but at the end only a small part of the total. Over the course of the 16 years spanning 1992–2005, one of us conducted 30 time management seminars called *Priorities, Planning and* Paperwork.[23] Delegates were asked to keep a schedule of how they had spent the previous week, and the results averaged over all these seminars for clergy was:

21%	Administration
19%	Time with family
14%	Meetings
14%	Study and preparation
12%	Other duties (often outside the church)
11%	Services
9%	Visiting people and pastoral work

Whether this is how ministers *should* spend their time is for discussion; this is how over 500 clergy *had* spent their time. The issues of priorities, keeping the main thing the main thing, work/life balance and focusing on their vision are all part of this mix. Few were satisfied with the breakdown that they saw, and many felt that a day a week on administration was too much.

Do not ministers face much pressure? Yes, they do, partly because of the imbalance between perceived priorities and actual work. The urgent often took the place of the important. One worn-out minister had had to do six funerals in 10 days! Time and values are always the critical components of which action to undertake next: *when* must it be done by, *who* wants it done? One survey put the top four pressures as: Internal administration (70%), External bureaucracy (60%), Under-financing (58%) and Lack of skilled leaders (53%).[24]

Multiple churches

One element of such pressure may be seen in the fact that some ministers are responsible for more than one church. The record is probably held by the vicar in the Church of England Diocese of Norwich who had 15 churches, but that is at the extreme end! One piece of research in the late 1980s found that looking after more than four churches at a time diminished a minister's competence to effect real change, but some senior leaders wonder whether this is still true with modern communications.[25]

The 2005 English Church Census asked ministers how many churches they were responsible for, and the answers were as follows,[26] giving an average of 1.9 churches per minister:

68%	1 church
10%	2 churches
7%	3 churches
6%	4 churches
3%	5 churches
2%	6 churches
2%	7 churches
1%	8 or 9 churches, and
1%	10 or more churches.

The average number varied significantly by denomination with the Anglicans the most (3.3 each), followed by the Methodists (3.0) and then the United Reformed Church (2.1) and the Orthodox (2.0).

Training of ministers

An interesting study was published in 1990 which looked at the *outcome* of the training that was expected after ministers had attended theological college.[27] The study identified which model of ministry was anticipated, and measured each college in two ways – the percentage which identified with each at all, and the degree of importance associated with each, the latter marked on a scale from one to five. The results are summarized in Table 7.

Table 7   *Models of Ministry, and the importance given to them in training, 1990*

Model	Outcome	Identified with model %	Priority given to model (1 = high; 5 = low)
Preacher	As encourager of the faithful	87	2.4
Master	As knowledgeable teacher of the faith	86	3.1
Practical Theologian	As one who brings into a single focus the Church's thinking and practice	55	3.1
Priest	As representative of God and His people	43	3.2
Builder	As church grower	81	3.4
Manager	As facilitator of the Church's life and service	79	4.1
Therapist	As pastoral consultant	76	4.1

In terms of priority, all colleges gave priority to preaching (although Church of England colleges had the smallest percentage). The minister as master, practical theologian, priest, and builder were given similar priority overall, but this too varied by denomination. The Church of England colleges tended to stress being a practical theologian and priest, the Catholic colleges being a priest, and the other denominational and interdenominational colleges being a master and builder. Although identifying with the minister as manager and therapist, no college really gave this high priority. It would be intriguing to know how far these findings have changed over the last 20 years!

Growth by age and length of ministry

An important question that is often asked by ministers is, 'When should I move on?' One survey answered this question in terms of length of ministry by growth of the church. The proportion of Church of England churches which grew when the incumbent had been present for:[28]

1 to 4 years was	17%
5 or 6 years was	21%
7 to 9 years was	24%
10 to 13 years was	22%
14 to 17 years was	20%
18 or more years was	15%.

This suggests that the '10-year itch' that some ministers have is perhaps about right. Their church was most likely to grow after being present for between seven and nine years by which time the congregation had got to know the minister well, and hopefully the minister knew the congregation well. Some ministers have over-stayed their welcome and in their last five years have undone all the good done in the previous 15.

Some ministers successfully stay on for many years, however. The secret of such success is almost certainly whether or not after leading the church (or any organization for that matter) for say eight or 10 years, the leader can find a fresh vision to challenge the church for the years ahead. Where they can, let them stay; where they cannot, it really is time to move on!

An analysis of growth by age of minister is also interesting; the results, from the same study, are shown in Figure 3.

Figure 3 Church growth by age of incumbent, 1989–98

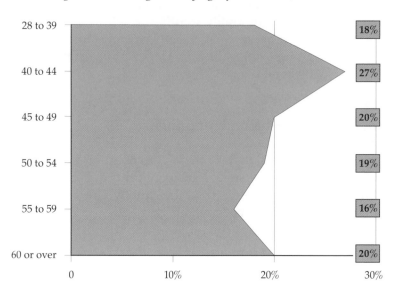

There are two ages where growth is most likely – when ministers are in their 40s or their 60s. This research was specific to the Church of England but the 2005 English Church Census found that it was also true for other denominations for the early 40s age, though not the early 60s. One person commented about clergy in their 60s: 'they know now they will not be given a residential canonry, nor become an Archdeacon or Bishop; they have their freehold, so they can hang the hierarchy and get on with it!', which apparently quite a number do!

Figure 3 also highlights a danger, however. During their 50s a minister can become increasingly disillusioned with things 'not working', which can lead to considerable frustration. An unpublished Church of England report made available to Bishops suggested that those over 50 should have an optional vocational assessment to help them assess their way forward in ministry.[29]

Perhaps the dip in the late 50s partly explains an increasing number of resignations in that period.[30]

Other factors

Much other research has been undertaken on ministerial life, including looking at their views on moral questions of the day, ecclesiastical government, matters of social concern, as well as personal elements such as how well they cope with the finance they receive, their personal goals, attitudes to worship and witness, signs of stress, etc. Ultimately, however, the authors of this chapter believe that ministerial wellbeing is concerned with the strength of their leadership, and their ability to energize and enable others to follow them. Two instances of this come from the book *Back from the Brink* which highlights churches which might have vanished had it not been for the minister.[31]

A Methodist/Anglican church in Liverpool was the last remaining voluntary organization on an outer city 'sink' estate. Two successive three-year part-time appointments of Church Army Captains had kept it alive, but without a dedicated, long-term, full-time leader the dwindling elderly congregation was losing the battle against vandalism, apathy and lack of resources. When Captain Phil Clarke and his family arrived they moved onto the estate rather than living in the 'nicer' end of the parish, and put their children into the local schools. They committed themselves to finding out what kind of ministry would be appropriate in this place, and to staying until they'd made a difference.

They soon started a KidzKlub, providing not only somewhere for local youngsters to go but fresh ideas and values for them to live by. The concept combines an action-packed programme at the weekly club meeting, including games and competitions as well as singing Christian songs and the telling of Bible stories. Alongside the club programme, leaders visit the home every week of each child who is registered. It took huge amounts of energy and dogged perseverance, much of it supplied by Phil and his wife and helped by those in neighbouring churches and the community itself who became excited by their vision. Parents soon began to recognize their weekly visitors and to start to trust them. In a surprisingly short time up to 350 children were attending, and as the months passed local people began to think of it as 'their church'. As the children grew too old for KidzKlub an older group was established for them, and some began to attend other church activities and services. Phil's efforts have been widely acknowledged and he has recently been appointed the programme leader of the Xplore Church Army programme for training young adults – but he'll still be based in his community in Liverpool.[32]

An Assemblies of God church in Southsea near Portsmouth has been turned around in a similar way by Gareth Benton, a visionary young leader who, when he first arrived at the church aged 21 found he had to do everything – the elderly congregation were supportive but unable to be very active. His vision was to develop all kinds of links into the local community, and over several years this included the Sure Start programme, mentoring in schools, and computer training as well as a thriving KidzKlub. So many new people came to the church that they first of all moved out of their old hall into a shopping area, and then had to rebuild to provide more space and meet current health and safety regulations. Some of their earliest KidzKlub members now help to lead the children's work and university students regularly commit themselves to Gareth's vision of making church 'work' in a run-down neighbourhood.

So what does all this say?

Ministers are crucial for the wellbeing and indeed survival of the churches in our land where attendance is falling fast. While numbers of ministers overall are relatively static, some denominations, particularly those involved in starting new congregations, have seen an increase over the last few years.

The average age of a minister is 54, about the same as adult members of their congregations, with as many under 50 as over 60. Again this varies by denomination, with especially the Roman Catholics, Independents and Orthodox having much higher proportions of older men. Some, like the Church of England, are ordaining more older people than 10 years ago.

One minister in seven, 15 per cent, is female, a percentage which is steadily increasing. The Salvation Army have the highest percentage, followed by the United Reformed Church and the Methodists. Fewer than average female ministers are responsible for city centre or suburban churches, and more than would be expected are in remoter rural areas. Churches with more than 300 attending on a Sunday are, thus far, looked after only by male ministers.

The churchmanship of a minister varies especially by gender, with fewer Catholic or Evangelical female ministers, and therefore a much larger proportion of those who are Broad or Liberal. Their belief system consequently reflects their churchmanship variations.

Ministers are usually called upon to lead. A third, 31 per cent, have specific leadership skills which emerge when measured on a Belbin grid. Just under half of these are 'Shapers', that is, those whose drive, energy and vision usually mean that their churches grow. However, ministerial responsibility inevitably changes by the size of their church, with those guiding the largest churches in effect being like a Company Board Chairman! Many ministers, however, look after small churches and require the resource and tenacity skills associated with that role. Growth may come with the energy many have in their 40s, but older ministers who may have become frustrated in their ministry should not be overlooked.

All this means that unless quite radical change occurs, the leadership necessary to revive the church for the future may not only be lacking in some situations now, but may not be in place in the days ahead either. There is much man- and woman-power in the field, but it is by no means certain that they all have the right personality types and leadership skills to meet the opportunities and challenges of the future.

Bibliography

Belbin, Meredith, *Management Teams: Why They Succeed or Fail* (London: Heinemann-Butterworth, 1981).

Brierley, Peter, *Priorities, Planning and Paperwork* (Speldhurst: Monarch, 1992).

Brierley, Peter, *Pulling out of the Nosedive* (London: Christian Research, 2006).

Francis, L.J. and John V. Payne, 2002, 'The Payne Index of Ministry Styles (PIMS): Ministry Styles and Psychological Type among male Anglican clergy in Wales', *Research in the Social Scientific Study of Religion*, Vol. 13, 125–41.

Gibbs, Eddie, *I Believe in Church Growth* (London: Hodder & Stoughton, 1981).

Louden, Stephen and Professor Canon Leslie Francis, *The Naked Parish Priest: What Priests Really Think They're Doing* (London: Continuum, 2003).

Wasdell, David, *Deployment, Growth and Mission in the Church of England* (London: Urban Church Project, 1974).

Wraight, Heather and Pat Wraight, *Back from the Brink* (West Sussex: Verité; and London: Christian Research; 2006).

Both authors were Directors of Christian Research for many years until they retired in 2007. Dr Peter Brierley is now responsible for Brierley Consultancy and may be reached on peter@brierleyres.com; Heather Wraight may be reached on heatherinyork@btinternet.com.

Notes

1 Revised Authorized Version.
2 *Religious Trends*, No 7, 2007/2008, edited by Peter Brierley, Christian Research, London, 2007.
3 Numbers from the professional associations concerned for 2001, taken from relevant editions of the *Life Style Pocketbook*, Advertising Association, Henley-on-Thames, Oxon.
4 Great Britain, because no attendance figures are available for Northern Ireland. These figures taken from *Religious Trends*, No 7, Table 2.24.4 (op. cit.).
5 *Religious Trends*, No 7, Table 2.21.3 (op cit).
6 Louden, Stephen and Leslie Francis, *The Naked Parish Priest: What Priests Really Think They're Doing* (London: Continuum, 2003).
7 Figures for the 1990s taken from *Religious Trends*, No 3, 2002/2003, Table 2.21.1, with later figures from *Religious Trends* No 7, 2007/2008, Table 2.21.2 (op cit).
8 Definitions for some of these terms may be found in *Painting by Numbers*, Peter Brierley, Christian Research, London, 2005, Chapter 6.

9 Taken from *Religious Trends,* No 6, 2006/2007, edited by Peter Brierley, Christian Research, London, 2006, Table 5.15.

10 The counts for the different descriptions are given in full in Table 5.12.1 in *Religious Trends,* No. 6 (ibid.).

11 Taken from *Religious Trends,* No. 4, 2003/2004, edited by Peter Brierley (Christian Research, London, 2003), Table 12.3.3.

12 Op. cit. (*RT* 6, Item 9).

13 Taken from Table 5.5.2 in *Religious Trends,* No. 6 (op. cit.).

14 Published in two booklets *Believe it or not!* by Rev Robbie Low and Francis Gardom and *The Mind of Anglicans* by Peter Brierley (Christian Research and Cost of Conscience: London, 2003).

15 Belbin, Meredith, *Management Teams: Why They Succeed or Fail* (Heinemann-Butterworth: London, 1981) (but has been reprinted virtually every year since).

16 Published in *Quadrant* (Christian Research, London), January 1996, p. 6.

17 Published in *Quadrant* (Christian Research, London), January 1998, p. 1.

18 Survey undertaken for the Salvation Army, some aspects of which were published in *Leadership, Vision and Growing Churches* (Christian Research, London, 2003).

19 All columns except lay people.

20 Francis, L.J. and John V. Payne, 2002, 'The Payne Index of Ministry Styles (PIMS): Ministry Styles and Psychological Type among male Anglican clergy in Wales', *Research in the Social Scientific Study of Religion,* Vol. 13, pp. 125–41.

21 Wasdell, Rev David, *Deployment, Growth and Mission in the Church of England* (Urban Church Project, London), August 1974.

22 Gibbs, Rev Dr Eddie, *I Believe in Church Growth* (Hodder & Stoughton: London, 1981), p. 380.

23 Based on the book *Priorities, Planning and Paperwork* by Peter Brierley (Speldhurst: Monarch, 1992).

24 Op. cit. (*The Mind of Anglicans*, Item 14), p. 9.

25 *Multiple Parish Survey: More Than One Church,* Peter Brierley (MARC EuropeL London), MARC Monograph No. 27, April 1989.

26 Brierley, Peter, *Pulling out of the Nosedive* (Christian Research: London, 2006), p. 180.

27 Bunting, Ian, *The Places to Train,* A Survey of Theological Training in Britain (Kingham Hill Trust and MARC Europe: London, 1990).

28 Brierley, Peter, *Church Growth in the 1990s,* A Statistical Report (Christian Research: London in association with Springboard: Abingdon, Oxon, 2000).

29 Bunting, Ian, *The Places to Train*, A Survey of Theological Training in Britain (Kingham Hill Trust and MARC Europe: London, 1990).

30 *Frustration to Fulfilment: The final ten years of licensed ministry*, John Lee, Clergy Appointments Adviser, was circulated in draft form to bishops for publication later in 2007 by Church House, London; so a report in the *Church Times,* 29 June 2007.

31 Op. cit. (*RT* 7, Item 2), Figure 8.5.3.

32 Wraight, Heather and Pat Wraight, *Back from the Brink* (Verité: Goring-by-Sea, West Sussex, and Christian Research: London, 2006).

33 Article 'A different path', *idea*, July/August 2007, p. 15.

3

Counting the Cost ... and Paying It

Rev Dr Martyn Atkins

'I think God's calling me into ministry.'

'That's wonderful,' I reply to Sue, a 23-year-old student.

'Scary, too,' she says, and begins to tell me about her sense of God's call.

One of the privileges of being Principal of a Christian training college is talking with Christian people who are seeking God's will and way for their lives. Over the years I have had many earnest conversations with young adults like Sue, experiencing a call to Christian ministry and service, and trying to discern it properly. In very recent years, however, I note a difference in the conversations which I think is significant. To be sure, when expressing their sense of call young adults today, both female and male, are just as fervent and committed as ever they were. They are clear too that the call is probably 'for life' rather than for a few years and that it is full time rather than part time – that is, it involves their livelihood rather than their 'leisure' time. What, then, is the significant difference?

'Sue, have you thought about ordained ministry?'

'I knew you'd say that! I've thought about it lots but the prospect is just awful! I mean, I see what my minister does, and he's very nice, and I'm sure it's all worthwhile, but ... it's not me. I don't feel called to that. I don't think it will use the gifts God is giving me. Well ... I just can't do that!'

What is different about these people compared with their counterparts of even a few years ago is a greater level of antipathy towards ordained ministry as they have witnessed it and understand it.

As the conversation continues the problem deepens.

'Okay Sue. Tell me where you feel your gifts lie, and what sort of ministry you think you may be called to.'

And Sue – or it could equally be Sam – goes on to outline gifts like evangelism; a passion to get alongside and help people, particularly those on the edge or outside the Church; a desire to 'change the world'; and a willingness to work among communities where present Christian witness is often most weak and ineffective. In short, with some irony, what they feel they can offer is just the kind of ministry the Christian Church needs in our increasingly post-Christendom context. Which, of course – because God is raising up people to minister in our cultural context – is not very surprising. In fact it's a sign of future hope – as long as the Church responds to such people properly and listens to the Spirit closely.

At this point in the conversation about God's call my own problem as mentor deepens. I am faced with a dilemma. Do I encourage the person to consider ordained ministry in a historic church like my own, or not? Certainly I can begin to gently point out to Sue/Sam that what they offer is not at all at odds with a proper understanding of ordained ministry. It isn't hard to make the case.

Demographically I can point out that (in my own Methodist Church, but it is true of other historic denominations also) the number of those offering for ordination is falling. I can draw attention to the fact that in spite of continuing – if slowing – numerical decline, my Church needs more (not less) folk entering holy orders than are currently offering in order to maintain current levels of ordained ministry. I can also make clear that the evidence suggests that alongside the modest numbers offering, a sizeable proportion of ordained active ministers will retire over the next decade, causing an ever-widening gap between need and provision to occur. And if, pray God, the Church does not continue to shrink but begins to grow a little through becoming more mission minded, then the big gap simply gets bigger unless it is overtaken by an accompanying upsurge in offers for ordination. Why is it such a surprise then that God might be calling people like them into ordained ministry 'at such a time as this'?

Theologically I can point out to Sue/Sam that their emphasis on mission-shaped church is just what is needed today. Being people-centred and community-focused is just right. I can often tell them that I recognize in them the gifts they articulate about themselves, that I bear witness to their call. And as for being willing to start a church in a house or hall in a housing estate in an inner city, well, the Church is crying out for such servanthood. Consequently I can assure them that there is nothing about their sense of call and giftedness which is inconsistent with ordained ministry. So what are we all waiting for?

But however easy it is to match a sense of call with the practical needs of the denomination and a broad theology of ordained ministry, I find it increasingly hard to do so. One reason is that I have, over the years, made such a case and thus persuaded some Sues and Sams that the ordained ministry *is* a proper route for them. They have subsequently undertaken the denominational processes and been declined, or told to come back later. In some cases the selectors were right, but in other cases one is led to the conclusion that the processes involved are mismatched to the nature of the offer of ministry, yet the offer of ministry is of a perfectly proper pattern for the Church today – and increasingly tomorrow.

In some other cases Sue/Sam was accepted for training for ordination and, while often experiencing fulfilment and stimulation while training, remained warily of the opinion that they were a round peg in a square system. In my experience, however it is the actual experience of exercising ministry in a 'normal' pastoral setting, rather than initial ministerial training, which is often found to be the most negative aspect. It is at this point when, for several young ministers I have known, various powerful forces combine to produce a life and ministry shaped too much like what they feared in the first place. They found it unappealing then, and their practical experience of it does not alter their mind.

Unless all this is a figment of my imagination, though the contents of this book suggests it is not, it is worth reflecting why, in recent years, some Sues/Sams have come to a more negative view of ordained ministry, and why comparatively few venture down that path.

One factor is surely that the role and expectations of ordained ministers have changed in certain respects. For example, the increasing need to undertake or oversee administrative and bureaucratic procedures such as employment legislation, safeguarding, health and safety audits, possibly complaints and grievance processes and the like, is well known and acknowledged. There is growing evidence nowadays that such functions are being undertaken by qualified lay workers, in a conscious attempt to lift from ordained ministers an over-preponderance of such things, enabling them to focus more fully upon 'what they were ordained to do'. It remains the case however that the lifestyle and expectations of much contemporary ordained ministry leave Sues / Sams distinctly underwhelmed.

Related to the above is the significant increase in lay posts advertised and appointed in local churches in recent years. A cursory glance in the major Church newspapers and Christian magazines reveals a plethora of youth, children's, family, neighbourhood, and pastoral worker posts to be had. Compared to previous generations, there are quite simply many more opportunities to work formally for God in God's Church. Not all are permanent and well paid to be sure, but since when has high remuneration been associated with Church ministry of any kind? One significant effect of the increase of such roles is to remove from ordained ministers a high level of involvement in ministries such as these. In many cases nowadays contact with young people, young adults, or families, is undertaken by the lay worker rather than the ordained minister. Other knock-on effects then pertain. The opinion that ordained ministry is primarily concerned with roles and tasks thought to be routine by comparison with such exciting 'hands on' ministries is reinforced. Many young people naturally aspire to become youth pastors, etc. giving back to that model of ministry which has given them so much, with obvious ramifications for the number of those open to offering for ordained ministry.

A further factor is that a significant proportion of young adults who feel called into ministry (lay or ordained) have not been evangelized and nurtured by 'inherited churches'. Yet such churches remain the 'normal' environment for most ordained appointments. A combination of the reduced contact with children and young people by many local churches, the huge rise in numbers going to universities and colleges (which remain fertile environments for evangelism, community and nurture through student groups of varying kinds), and the increase of Emerging Churches/fresh expressions/youth congregations and the like, combine to produce the fact that far fewer potential candidates for ordination have grown up in an inherited church context. At its starkest this means that a good proportion of younger people offering for ordination are offering significant experience, but experience of a quite different ecclesial world than that into which most are sent!

Yet another factor is the rising age profile of those offering for ordained ministry in most inherited Church denominations. There was a time when to be over 25 was to be too old to offer for the Methodist ministry, and not all that long ago. Now the 'average' candidate for ordination is as likely to be female as male, but both are likely to be in their 40s. Such folk bring lots of experience and in recent years this has arguably had an effect upon what selection panels look for and expect in candidates. It is simply the case that many 22-year-old males appear somewhat 'raw' when interviewed alongside mature women and men, articulate and experienced in terms of family, responsibility and considerable church association. Ironically, therefore younger candidates appear 'not ready' and inexperienced more than perhaps they once did. But inexperienced at what? As we have just noted, often inexperienced about 'normal' church, though not necessarily inexperienced in relation to exercising leadership among (student) groups, planting churches, organizing evangelistic events and processes, and initiating fresh expressions of church and patterns of Emerging Church. Nor are many contemporary young adults inexperienced of 'life', but rather 'life' of a different sort to that experienced by many adults of older generations, 'life' deemed to be proper and acceptable life experience required by the Church. The life experiences of young adults today resonates more easily than that of earlier generations for millions of people in our society, so that rather than dismiss different life experiences as largely irrelevant for the ministry we have in mind, we come to see such experience as crucial for authentic Christian ministry in the emerging future.

It is worth noting too that older candidates more naturally tend to emerge out of inherited church contexts, just as younger candidates may not. Similarly, older candidates understandably tend to sense a call to be a minister much like the ministers of the churches they emerge from. The models of ministry which switch off numbers of potential younger candidates resonate better with many older candidates. Consequently it might be argued that the higher numbers of older candidates for ministry unwittingly emphasizes a conservative, *status quo* view of ministry, but one increasingly at variance with the aspirations and experiences of many younger candidates.

We must focus a little more upon styles of leadership. The fact is that younger adults have been educated differently than earlier generations, and tend to express commitment, belonging and 'ownership' differently than earlier generations. Commitment is usually demonstrated by active participation rather than more passive support by simply being present. Faith needs to be lived out in order to be real and sustainable. To be worth being committed to, it must make a difference. These 'natural' expressions of commitment and leadership for younger people do not always fit easily into churches where a more settled arrangement of the role of the minister and the responsibilities of the laity are unquestioned and sustained.

Consequently many young people exercise a subtly different model of leadership than that naturally expressed by inherited church processes and expectations. It is not that younger people are inherently against 'facilitating' or 'theological reflection', but many of them put a higher store on explicit leadership, envisioning, and the spiritual authority and expectations of the role.

The 'cost' of all this should be, by now, obvious. Even allowing for the stark and hyperbolic presentation given here, there are enormous ramifications arising from the situation outlined above.

How are we to proceed?

1. There is a clear need for improved patterns of discerning God's call among young adults. This will include a broader

and better means of assessing their life experiences and the nature of their discipleship and commitment. It will also involve a more nuanced means of understanding leadership, and discerning aptitude for ministry in – and for – a changing cultural context.

2. Identifying and accepting a greater variety of focuses of call, within ordained ministry, is also crucial. The Church of England has recently begun to explore ministry 'tracks' for those experiencing a call to various kinds of different ministries within the whole ministry of the Church – sometimes referred to as 'pioneer ministries', though not all such are necessarily pioneering. Other denominations must explore such 'tracks' as a matter of urgency, not because we need to find appropriately shaped 'holes' for those we admit to ordination to fill, but because we discern with increasing clarity that God is calling new kinds of minister for new contexts of ministry.

3. A robust assessment of what this means in terms of initial ministerial training – and what it doesn't – needs to be worked through. I have long been a supporter of the understanding of theology and understanding of ministry outlined by Ellen Charry in her fine book *By the Renewing of Your Minds: The Pastoral Function of Christian Doctrine* (OUP, 1997). Put simply, as part of a complicated but persuasive thesis, she argues that in the Patristic era theology arose naturally as the Church engaged in being the Church, in much the same way that Martin Kahler argued that theology arises as a natural consequence of mission. That is, proper theology is the reflection and outworking of the life of the Church and the deepening of faith and discipleship by those who belong in it. To misquote Cyprian, *extra ecclesiam nulla theologica* (outside the Church there is no theology)! Consequently, much of what is understood to be 'theology' over the last 200 years would probably not be recognized as such by the Patristic leaders of the Church. Put sharply, true theology is not that which is taught in universities or by those uncommitted to what they teach, standing outside the *ecclesia* of Christ, but rather that which is taught and embodied by those who stake their lives on what they teach. This approach takes us beyond silly questions about whether ministerial training

contains too much or too little theology in the sense that the nature and aim of theology itself is revised.

My own view is that a move to revisit such 'true theology' within the pastoral office and its call to ordained leadership in the contemporary church holds far more hope for the future for us all – not just young adults – than perpetuating a system of training for ordination that persists with the view that its key aim is to create 'mini theologians' of a certain, modernist kind. Such integrated, practical, whole-life, missional theology resonates profoundly with many contemporary candidates for ordination, and not least younger adults.

4. Revisiting, appropriately revising, and innovatively imple-menting new means of mentoring by selected and trained mentors is vital.

A piece of research undertaken some years ago by Leslie Francis on behalf of the Anglican Church in Wales is helpful here. Francis was asked to investigate a high proportion of fallout of clergy in the first few years of active ministry. Why was this happening? Not surprisingly, Francis concluded this was down to a number of factors, but one was unexpected and significant. He discovered that the decision 'not to spend the rest of my life doing this' was made quite quickly, sometimes within months or a couple of years of starting in the first parish. Two things were noted. First that entry into a parish was not, for many, a positive experience, and secondly that key to this crucial period of ministry was the relationship with the Rector or Vicar. Where good mentoring, training, support, and encouragement took place, the health and outlook of the minister was significantly better than in cases where no mentoring or good oversight took place. As a result, a key recommendation of Francis' report was that those clergy taking up oversight of those in first and second curacies should be carefully selected, as they held the key to the overall health and longevity of a new generation of clergy.

My instinct is to suggest that this is true not only of clergy in the Church of Wales! Indeed, a good number of young leaders I know have taken the initiative to find mentors, coaches and spiritual directors of various kinds, in consequence of a felt need for such support. Appropriate support structures for today are required with some urgency. Both younger and older candidates for ordination as well as the newly ordained would benefit.

5. Last but by no means least is the complex challenge of the expectations of many local churches, in terms of the nature of the ordained ministry. Means need to be found whereby the necessary 'space', 'authority' and 'permission' for different kinds of ordained ministries to be exercised is provided. At national, regional and local level we must begin to share the vision of a more variegated ministry in which ordination is an accepted locus. This will require management by national secretaries, by diocesan/district leaders, and encouragement and releasing of local leaders by deans, superintendent ministers and the like.

There will, no doubt, be local churches that continue to require and demand a 'traditional' ministry. But there are also, it seems to me, a fast-growing number of local churches where leading members of the congregation are themselves discerning the possibilities of new models of ministry. The 'mixed economy' of church spoken of by the Archbishop of Canterbury is increasingly with us. And for a mixed economy of church is required a mixed economy of ministry: lay and ordained, contextual, changing and flexible. In my book *Resourcing Renewal: shaping church for the emerging future* (Inspire, 2007) I outline how our changing cultural context requires both 'new ministry' and 'new laity' because, quite simply, the laity who populate many of our churches today are quite different human beings from those who have faithfully belonged to our churches for generations past.

Sues and Sams are being called and prepared for ordained ministries today. My prayer is that those of us who hold offices and roles in our churches will endeavour with greater passion and intent than ever to find better appropriate ways of discerning the call, training, forming, ordaining, mentoring, and releasing Sue and Sam for the ministry to which they are being called by God, now, here, among us.

4

Overcoming Theological Inertia

Steve Dutfield and Gordon Cotterill

In the 1970s and early 1980s industrial Great Britain faced an issue: shipbuilding, mining, the car industry, and the printing industry all struggled to exist in a world that was different. Memories of geography lessons and essays written about industrial inertia – the survival of an industry in an area even though the factors which led to its location there no longer apply – seem to make an odd connection with the concern of this chapter regarding Bible college leadership training. Bible colleges face their own issue of inertia as they struggle to survive in a world that is different.

Webber recalls a comment of a 'younger evangelical', which in many ways is representative of these issues: 'If you graduated from seminary before 1985, you were trained to lead a church that no longer exists.'[1]

Gibbs and McLaren further highlight and recognize the problem that this chapter seeks to address. Gibbs points out that 'The ministry training I received over forty years ago was for a world that now no longer exists, and even at the time was undergoing radical change'.[2] Similarly, McLaren underlines that perhaps some seminaries are still fighting the battles of yesterday, 'largely oblivious to the issues of today, hardly thinking of the issues of tomorrow'.[3]

There was a time when church life was simple. You knew, within an accepted range of difference, what to expect wherever you went. You were either traditional or you were radical. You either worshipped with the help of an organ or a three-piece band playing Graham Kendrick. It was either the hymnal or some contemporary hybrid. Training leaders for that world was not without its challenges, but these were mostly met with the tool bag of sound 'systematic theology' and hermeneutics.

It's not that simple any more. The chaos of diversity prevails and promises only to deepen. A taxonomy of ecclesiology now places 'traditional' alongside 'Pentecostal', 'seeker sensitive' alongside 'primitive', 'radical change' alongside 'post-evangelical' and even 'post-charismatic': a smorgasbord of Christian choice. In the midst of this kaleidoscopic culture and thought, Bible seminaries, schools and colleges are facing the challenge of preparing leaders.

Two big issues face the classic Bible college. Firstly, that of maintaining a credible learning environment within the demands of a postmodern and post-Christian society; secondly, that of the identification, resourcing and empowerment of leaders within a new generation.[4] In considering these issues, institutional training models will need to face up to the challenge of modelling transition such that faithfulness to Christian ministry is not sacrificed on the altar of relevance.

Webber, Gibbs and McLaren clearly indicate that the world that Bible schools generally trained church leaders for is changing and diversifying, and so is the Church. *Fresh expressions of church* would seem to be an all-embracing definition of this diversification of ecclesiology and could represent anything from church plants through to cell church; traditional forms of church inspiring new interest through to alternative worship communities; churches arising out of community initiatives through to school-based and school-linked congregations and churches.[5] Heath White makes the unsurprising observation that 'every institution is affected by the culture in which it lives and especially the culture in which it was born'.[6] The Bible college is no exception.

This chapter tries to offer dialogue by affirming that, although the world is changing, God's direction in people's lives to be partners in his mission remains constant. The concern of this chapter is first to offer context to the issues of incongruity that face Bible colleges. Building on this foundation we then move towards an analysis of some leadership training models before highlighting the dangers of 'jumping in with both feet' without asking the right questions.

Introducing David and Jane

David[7] was a part-time youth worker who had shown interest when I took up a new appointment looking after Mission Studies and Spiritual Formation at The Salvation Army's William Booth College in London. David's opinion was that I had sold out! No longer a local church leader working in spite of the institution, now I had become its representative. David with his jeans hanging off, his Calvin Kleins for all to see, his baseball hat at right angles, gave me something to consider. If God's direction was to be fulfilled through the ministry training college I represented, David would have to do a lot of conforming.

Elsewhere it has already been seen that there is a new generation of Davids and others like him. Jim Wallis, in his foreword to Shane Claiborne's *The Irresistible Revolution*, points out that '... perhaps the greatest sign of hope is the emergence of a new generation of Christians eager and ready to take their faith into the world'.[8]

But the world is not just made up of Davids. Later that afternoon I was engaged in another conversation. Rather than being seen as the guardian of the institution, I now stood accused of embodying all that is perceived as 'emerging', a threat to all things traditional. I listened to the perception, the near anger as Jane expressed her view.[9] Her need is for clearer guidelines, firmer control and stronger maintenance of traditional values. Jane's diatribe concluded in exasperation: '*You are here to tell us how and what to think....*' Jane's passion, longing and drive was coming from a good place, a deep desire to serve God through church, to engage in mission and ministry.

A chasm connected through 'calling'

David and Jane are seemingly a chasm apart, but connected through one sense of calling. David is one of Webber's 'younger evangelicals', no doubt having a strong sense of God's direction and calling on his life, with no compromise to the urgency that is his to live and love out the gospel. The only compromise for him is what he sees and understands of the Bible college form of missional equipping. As Roxburgh identifies

Many of these people are no longer willing to jump through denominational hoops in order to be recognized as leaders. They believe such hoops no longer make sense in today's world. For them, seminary (or 'cemetery' as some mockingly refer to it) education is suspect. It seems so distant and abstract. It demands that students be uprooted and placed in an unreal, disassociated, ivory tower environment for several years – only to end up serving in settings where, once again, they have no previous relationship.[10]

Jane and those like her also share a strong sense of God's direction and calling with no compromise to the urgency that is theirs to live and love out the gospel. The only compromise for the Janes is what they see as an unnecessary relaxation of traditional values.

Whereas Jane would show a discomfort with individuality, she would be comfortable with jumping through the hoops in order to train for ministry and mission; conversely David would feel abhorrence at the structured institutionalism that would seemingly threaten his individuality. Nevertheless, not only do they share a similar sense of God's direction and guidance, the same desire to serve God, and a similar depth of understanding of mission – they also potentially share the same context in which their training is worked out. It is from this that we move on to look at a variety of ministry-training options.

Between Athens and Berlin

There can be little doubt that the opportunities are enormous. A glance through the *UK Christian Handbook* for 2007–8 lists well over one hundred colleges offering training for anyone interested in Christian ministry.[11] Even more widespread opportunities exist in the United States. Robert Banks, writing in the late 1990s suggests that two hundred and seventy-five institutions were affiliated with the Association of Theological Schools together with several times as many Bible institutes, training schools, and lay theological centres as well as some substantive para-church or church-based ventures in theological education.[12] The existence of both residential and non-residential training, of full-time or

part-time training, of validated and non-validated courses suggests that the Church has become open to a huge variety of training methods in order to encourage as many people as possible to find some form of suitable training for their chosen vocation.

Before considering the specific nature of training available today, it might be helpful to highlight a concept suggested by David Kelsey in his work considering the nature of theological education in the United States in the late twentieth century. He coined the phrase 'between Athens and Berlin' to describe the two possible paradigms which undergird the training opportunities which currently exist.

> Within an exclusively Athens community, teachers and students would normally share a similar faith commitment, sharing in community worship with spiritual development an aim for both. An underlying faith commitment would be assumed for both parties. Within an exclusive Berlin community, adherence to a faith position might not be evident; attendance at communal worship would be optional and be subject to critical study. The role of the teacher would be to develop critical scholarship amongst the student body.[13]

Whilst acknowledging that theological education is *between* Athens and Berlin, it appears that a leaning towards Berlin seems to have been favoured by a number of Bible colleges, as the desire for validated qualifications has become sought after. We wonder if this is an issue for those seeking to follow God's call today. Could it be that those called by God to church leadership would value an even more explicit Athens mode of training, whilst perceiving (albeit often mistakenly) the training on offer to be one which is in Berlin mode?

Gibbs points out that 'the primary reference point of graduate schools, of which seminaries are one type, is to meet the academic requirements of accrediting agencies',[14] and we understand that this might be a cause of considerable tension. We wonder if the requirements of academia are driving Christian training in a way which is inconsistent with its purpose for existing. Accreditation doesn't appear to have increased student numbers, so if its purpose was to give credibility and to encourage prospective students, it clearly hasn't worked.

Webber warns of the problem: 'While our educational institutions are rising in intellectual stature, they are decreasing in influence.'[15] Have we actually lost the art of building institutions which transform society? Have our colleges moved so far towards Berlin that we have lost sight of Athens? It is an issue which Bible colleges need to face up to as they consider their place in today's qualification-driven world. This call for qualified people has to be tempered by the need for Christian leaders to have an authentic and developing faith. Perhaps in the world of Christian ministerial training you can't be in Berlin without first ensuring you have a foot firmly planted in Athens.

So what are the options?

The residential option

The full-time, residential model is still favoured by many. This affords the opportunity to spend time 'set apart' with like-minded people studying the subject areas which will be of help in ministry whilst reflecting on the past, present and potential future spiritual journey to be made.

There are clear advantages to this type of training. It allows for information to be passed on and assessed through regular and rigorous assignments. It gives opportunity for any sense of calling to be tested and some idea of spiritual development to be discerned. It also allows for the monasterial living which McLaren suggests will be fundamental to the seminaries of the future.[16]

It encourages the multi-generational approach advocated by some.[17] As people are following the 'call' to ministry at various stages of life, a mutual enriching of the learning experience of all students seems to be occurring.

The placement-based option

It is worth noting the significance of the mission agency aspect of training referred to by McLaren.[18] In a recent article concerned with the changing nature of training at Bristol Baptist College, it was noted that all ministerial students would be sent on mission trips overseas. By discovering something of the nature of working in different settings, students' experience would be broadened, and theological reflection would be encouraged *in situ*. The Principal, the Rev Dr Stephen Finamore says, 'I wanted to give what we do a more missional edge [...]. Rather than getting the idea that their job is to manage decline, I want them [Bristol students] to have an idea that there is more to it than that'.[19]

Perhaps Gibbs has it right when he says, 'We need to move beyond *theology of mission* as a separate discipline to a *missional theology* that affects the seminary curriculum as a whole'.[20] One of the ways in which this shift to a more missional mindset is happening is by a bringing together of theory and practice.

In referring to the publication *Higher Education and Work-based Learning*, Brenda Little says, 'The government is currently putting increasing emphasis on higher education institutions engaging with employers in relation to teaching and learning'.[21] Placement-based learning is recognized in a number of professions, as for example with the school-centred Initial Teacher Training for those wishing to embark on a teaching career.

Increasingly it would seem that considerable numbers of people are following a route to church leadership which does not involve a residential course. Gibbs and Coffey suggest that 'most mainline denominations are training far more people for ministry on part-time or church-based courses than on full-time'.[22] It is suggested that in some traditions 80 per cent of student ministers are following a placement-based approach. For The Salvation Army in the UK this figure stands at about 20 per cent.

Although not claiming to be a theological college, Forge is a mission training network established in Australia.[23] For them, actional context is vital to learning, applying this not only to their missiological agenda, but also to leadership and ministry as a whole. Taking people slightly out of their comfort zone and then bringing the learning to them is fundamental to their philosophy. Learning with Forge consists of placements punctuated by intensive study blocks, the contents of which are determined by the needs of the students. As a consequence, learning is geared to fit the pressing needs of the student, arising out of the real situations they are confronted with in ministry, their learning being enhanced by their placement. Frequent coaching is fundamental to their approach, together with inspirational teaching delivered by practitioners, encouraging students to be imaginative in the ways they understand missional church.

But this type of training is not exclusive to the Antipodes. The summary of the report *Faithful Cities* includes the importance of relevant training for anyone seeking to serve in the context of urban ministry. They suggest that 'opportunities for training and development in urban ministry, lay and ordained, should be fully integrated into the churches' formal training and accreditation and, wherever possible, be done ecumenically'.[24] There are certainly moves to increase ecumenical opportunities for learning. Although much of this happens through non-denominational Bible colleges, there are formal arrangements for learning to take place in an ecumenical setting. In the United Kingdom inter-denominational partnerships are well established.[25]

But what might be the appeal of a practitioner-based model? 'What *Faithful Cities* usefully raises is the absolute necessity for getting a better grip on integrating theology and experience.'[26] Younger evangelical David Clark says, 'Information without transformation is pointless'.[27] The fear of a disconnect between what is taught and how it works out in practice is, it would seem, widespread. There needs to be a deliberate attempt at marrying theory and experience and that one without the other will simply not do for the potential leaders of today.

A number of opportunities for developing this placement-based approach are available, particularly to encourage and mobilize the laity. St Helen's, Bishopgate (in London) utilizes an associate scheme, setting out to 'help to develop the next generation of servant-leaders'.[28] Training takes place through classroom-based activities as well as by learning 'on the job'. St Helen's is deeply committed to this scheme, not only for the benefit of the Anglican Church, but for any who are seeking to go into full-time Christian ministry.

The Salvation Army has a number of Lieutenants who seem to be following a similar path. These people, who have not been ordained, are usually utilized by the Army in a local setting. Their training is minimal, but their understanding of local culture is impressive and quite possibly of greater importance.

We wonder if these two examples indicate a willingness on behalf of the Church to allow people to 'test the water', before plunging into a life of full-time service as both often lead to Bible college training. Could it be that these are instances of an approach which is trying to make training opportunities more flexible, whilst still holding to the methods of the past?

However, Michael Roberts expresses some important concerns with context-based learning.[29] Whilst acknowledging that it is a popular mode of learning in a number of professions, he suggests that there is something to be said for examining context from a distance, with a measure of theoretical understanding to help ground the reflection. And we have to agree that he has a point. When it works well it can work very well, but when it doesn't it can create a number of difficulties. There may be issues of accountability. What about time management? How does learning in one context translate to learning in other contexts in which the student might find themselves?

So how might there be a bringing together of the best of residential and placement-based training? The residential model offered at The Salvation Army Crestmont College in California has an interesting component.

> Taken in the last quarter of their second year, cadets are virtually assigned a corps to which they must relate – just as if they were the actual officer in charge of the corps. Cadets receive daily scenarios and have virtual divisional commanders that they relate to. All of the situations they deal with have actually happened in the West.[30]

Perhaps this is what Gibbs and Coffey hint at.

> [S]eminary and theological courses need to contain surprise elements … in the midst of learning about biblical, systematic and historical theology, students need to be presented with contemporary problems to test their ability to contextualise and apply what they are learning.[31]

Maybe this is where the positives of residential learning can be enjoyed and the practicalities of experience undertaken from the safety of a desk, in front of a computer terminal where mistakes can be made without the danger of messing things up long term for real people.

Any other options?

During the early eighteenth century some of the prime movers in the Great Awakening were the 'home schooled' preachers. Despite having enemies from the traditional academic institutions of the day they became the triggers of that great revival. Tony Campolo suggests a possible adaptation of this today.

> With distance-learning programs and the Internet, such candidates need not set foot on a seminary campus, yet they can acquire all the subject matter they'd receive in a traditional seminary experience. Add practical experience and mentoring by a seasoned pastor, and home training of this sort could be the best option for the education of many ministers.[32]

One wonders if this involves actively seeking out lay leaders, training them in their own context, using those familiar with that context to carry out the training. As Donald Miller suggests, 'When it is time to hire a new staff member, for example, perhaps someone should be selected from the ranks of the laity. Why? Because that person has proven his or her leadership abilities and fully understands the vision and culture of the institution.'[33]

Mission-Shaped Church highlights the need to recognize the significance of lay leadership. It suggests that 'if the missionary challenge we face is to be met, many new initiatives will be lay led'.[34] Indeed, 'The critical factor will be our ability to identify and train emerging leaders in context'.[35] Is this culturally relevant training at its best?

There is also a deliberate desire to encourage lay leadership in the development of their gifts and skills so as to best serve the Church. Courses such as CPAS' *Growing Leaders* is one means of developing leaders *in situ*, whilst allowing them opportunities to take time out and reflect on their practice with the help of a mentor.[36] 'Crucible' is offered over three weekends, encouraging those who are called to planting new expressions of church.[37] This training, coupled with placements, allows opportunities for learning and developing skills for such new expressions. 'Resource: Creating Church in the Emerging Culture' is a similar venture.[38] Over five weekends students engage in active learning, based on their placement experiences in order to

- be equipped to create church in the emerging culture;
- develop mission strategies for their specific context;
- explore and apply skills in leadership and discipleship;
- develop capacity for spiritual and personal growth.

These are bold claims, but it could be that this course too is offering opportunities for people who would probably bypass the traditional training establishments.

Clearly any consideration of the methods of training available today cannot ignore the easy availability of internet-based resources. There are countless websites inviting potential students to develop their skills for ministry. One such site is

http://mintools.com,

where there are many different ways in which a prospective church leader can develop further the gifts and skills they have. The opportunities to graduate through online universities abound. Another site,

www.worldwidelearn.com/online-degrees//index.html

is an example of this wealth of opportunity. Of course, it goes without saying that some of these sites should come with a health warning as a discerning eye needs to be cast over the material.

In concluding this section, it is worth noting that as with most things, edges are becoming increasingly blurred. We have tried to make a distinction between residential and placement-based training alternatives. We have acknowledged that the options are considerable, but we also need to note that it may not be that simple. There is an element of the residential and the placement-based in most courses.

This exemplifies some of the difficulty in giving clear options concerning training for David or Jane today. Some could be seen as more 'individualistic' while others are more 'institutional'. So what models should the institutional churches be looking to embrace? Perhaps a consideration of one further concept would help.

The tension of *Communitas*

The eighteenth-century French politician Charles-Maurice de Talleyrand is quoted to have said: 'Without individuals nothing happens, without institutions nothing survives.'[39] David and Jane can offer each other an alternative to training that brings counterbalance. For training and seminaries to be dominated by 'individualism' could lead to a loss of a common sense in the priorities of theology and practice. A real danger of a training that embraces rampant individualism would be that experimentation would always lead to further experimentation without facing the real issues of training within an era of transition. Equally for seminaries to remain bastions of 'institution' would dilute a church leadership that needs to act decisively and effectively.

With the words of Talleyrand ringing clear regarding 'institutions' and 'individualism', Sandercock-Brown points out that 'neither is appealing, but embrace the tension – that is something else'.[40] To embrace this tension between institution and individuality could offer a new source of creativity to train and equip Christian leaders for ministry.

Roxburgh suggests that when faced with 'discontinuous change' there are two responses.[41] 'There are those that attempt to return or recreate the organization's prior traditions, habits and way of life', or 'there are those that abandon the old and create a new future'. These two familiar tribes – already contextualized here within David and Jane – he terms 'Liminals' and 'Emergents'.

The Emergents, a collection of younger leaders who have little sense of loyalty to the denominational systems of the past,

> are deeply suspicious of the value of the educational systems of the past. They are deeply suspicious of the value of the educational systems set up in the 20th century to prepare leaders for the Church and have an almost reflexive reaction to anything they identify as the institutional Church.[42]

Liminals are guided by a framework shaped by loyalties that lie within church systems which flourished in the past. They are steeped in tradition and orthodoxy, feeling a sense of loss when faced with fresh expressions and new frameworks. However, Liminals and Emergents, with differing degrees of motive and enthusiasm, would agree with Roxburgh when he points out: 'The development and training of leaders requires more than traditional seminary programmes.'[43]

The obvious trend would be isolation from one another in terms of training. We have noted the burgeoning of validated courses on offer from a wide variety of sources. While attractive to our 'pick and mix' emerging culture, their isolation is a weakness. David would quite happily accept such training but would be isolated from Jane; equally Jane would have no reason with which to rub shoulders with David. 'Never the twain shall meet', theologically, would have implications in preparing leaders for ministry for a world and Church in transition. Such an isolationist approach is a significant weakness.

Borrowing from anthropology Roxburgh introduces the concept of *Communitas* as a place of potential and discovery where people collide and discover one another on a very different level of identity and role. It makes sense that within the storms of transition the Church is navigating, there is a need for Emergents to reconnect with Liminals. Issues can then be embraced together and the confusion that faces the Church in its ministry and mission may be countered.

Ministerial training colleges, if they are to send out leaders who are able to move beyond their own partisan approach to ministry and mission, need to embrace the tension between individuality and institution and encourage an environment of creativity through a process of dialogue and understanding. This comes through recognizing the importance that both Liminals and Emergents have much to offer each other in *Communitas*. Perhaps this is a positive call for both Liminals and Emergents to express their own individuality. As Jamison suggests: 'Individuality involves bringing your particular contribution to bear on the life of the community, even if that is a difficult contribution for others to accept'.[44]

Asking the right questions

It has been seen that the goalposts are shifting, causing a need for seminary programmes – in their ongoing struggle with their *raison d'être* – to adjust rapidly. However, if there is value for new and innovative ways of training to exist, the reasons for such innovation have to be secure. The foundational question is 'why change?'

Falling numbers of those entering ministry are denominationally unilateral. Within the context of The Salvation Army, the days of post-war Great Britain where those training to be commissioned as Salvation Army officers could be numbered in excess of 200, have fallen to a contemporary average of just over 30. Strategically this poses obvious questions of concern. However to proceed without asking the right questions would perpetuate the problem of the wrong framework for training rather that bring the necessary innovation.

Amidst these falling numbers there is a danger of missing the point that quick-fix solutions tend to ignore. Assuming that strategic plans are what will see seminaries and Bible colleges through, a temporary 'blip' could present a mistake born of asking the wrong question. The resultant cosmetic training product will remain one of attraction, of which the Emergent Davids would be deeply suspicious and the Liminal Janes would find quizzical.

As consideration and thought has been given to what models of training are required in the twenty-first century some of the right questions need to be asked in order to bring strength to the way forward. While it cannot be denied that the transition the Church and its training establishments find themselves in is profoundly disruptive, there are also great opportunities as a new generation of leaders emerges.

Asking the right questions mean that Bible colleges need to move away from being merely attractional to training being more missional in essence. Webber, through pointing out the demands of the contemporary shift of Bible college curricula from 'information to formation', suggests that if the development of Bible colleges is based on the wrong questions such Bible seminaries will be consigned to history. Therefore it is important to call into question a curriculum that reflects modernity; it is important to ask questions that will challenge a framework that lacks the context of culture; it is important to ask questions that highlight a lack of creativity and applicability; to question anything that continues to separate theology from practice and to question that which has lost its focus on wisdom, character and spiritual leadership as its goal.[45]

Conclusion

So to what we believe is the right and foundational question. The world is a rapidly changing place; however, God continues to call and direct a new generation of leaders with unprecedented passion for mission, beyond that of a 1980s euphemism for evangelism. But how do Bible colleges catch this wave of unparalleled opportunity to be part of a 'new generation of hope'? How do they do this when

> many young workers … find that they just do not fit in [when they] live under the constant strain of pretending to be who they are not in order to 'fit'; whilst others submit to the demands of the agency and become clones of their leaders devoid of freshness and innovative potential.[46]

Rather than simply fitting this new category of student into existing programmes, leaders of seminaries and new-paradigm churches need to sit down together to redesign curricula and course formats so that they will more adequately meet current needs.[47]

Responding to Campolo's thoughts on seminaries Brian McLaren says that he didn't attend seminary. One of the problems with such establishments is that they often

> recruit students who already know what they think and are not interested in having their thinking stretched or challenged, thank you very much … we teach them what to think, not how to think; or we obsessively teach them how to answer yesterday's questions while failing to face today's and or to anticipate tomorrow's.

As a consequence

> our brightest young Christians do not consider seminary (or, by implication, church ministry) an attractive place of worthwhile challenge.[48]

Perhaps the training of the future will incorporate some of McLaren's ideas:

- A more deliberate integration with the life of the local church
- An apprenticeship model
- Lifelong learning in dynamic learning communities
- The unfolding of the Christian story rather than analysis and systematics
- Sensitivity to contemporary cultural issues
- Global and missional settings
- Authentic spirituality
- Gender inclusiveness.[49]

We wonder if this is already happening – perhaps in response to the declining number of people offering for full-time service, maybe in a piecemeal fashion as new people are called, presenting new issues to be faced – but all, it is to be hoped, in a genuine attempt to have training which will authentically engage with both the Janes and Davids in this changing world.

Bibliography

Banks, Robert, *Reenvisioning Theological Education: Exploring a Missional Alternative to Current Models* (Grand Rapids, MI: Eerdmans, 1999).

Campolo, Tony, *Adventures in Missing the Point* (Grand Rapids, MI: Zondervan 2003).

Claiborne, S., *The Irresistible Revolution: Living As an Ordinary Radical* (Grand Rapids, MI: Zondervan, 2006).

Gibbs, E., *LeadershipNext: Changing Leaders in a Changing Culture* (Downers Grove, IL: InterVarsity Press, 2005).

Coffey, Ian and Eddie Gibbs, *ChurchNext: Quantum Changes in Christian Ministry* (Leicester: InterVarsity Press, 2001).

Cray, Graham, et al., *Mission-Shaped Church: Church Planting and Fresh Expressions of Church in a Changing Context* (London: Church House, 2004).

Grove, Daniel, *The Baptist Times*, 7 June 2007.

Jamison, A., *Finding Sanctuary: Monastic Steps for Everyday Life* (Collegeville, MN: Liturgical, 2006).

Kelsey, David H., *Between Athens and Berlin: The Theological Education Debate* (Grand Rapids, MI: Eerdmans, 1993).

Little, Brenda, 'Higher Education and work-based learning' in *Higher Education Digest*, Summer 2007, Issue 58.

McLaren, Brian D., *A New Kind of Christian: A Tale of Two Friends on a Spiritual Journey* (San Francisco, CA: Jossey-Bass, 2001).

Miller, Donald, *Reinventing American Protestantism: Christianity in the New Millennium* (Berkeley, CA: University of California, 1997).

New Frontier, The Salvation Army College for Officer Training at Crestmont, USA Western Territory.

Roberts, Michael, 'Thread in the Formation of Faithful Clergy' in *Contact: practical theology and pastoral care*: 152: Faithful Cities, 2007.

Roxburgh, A. J., *The Sky is Falling: Leaders Lost in Transition* (Eagle, IL: ACI, 2005).

Sandercock-Brown, G., 'Embrace the Tension' in *The Officer*, Jan/Feb 2006.

Tiplady, R. (ed.), *Postmission: World Mission by a Postmodern Generation* (Carlisle: Paternoster, 2002).

Webber, Robert, *The Younger Evangelicals: Facing the Challenges of the New World* (Grand Rapids, MI: Baker, 2002).

White, Heath, *Postmodernism 101: A First Course for the Curious Christian* (Grand Rapids, MI: Brazos, 2006).

Wilton, Gary, 'From ACCM22 to Hind via Athens and Berlin: A Critical Analysis of Key Documents Shaping Contemporary Church of England Theological Education with Reference to the Work of David Kelsey' in *Journal of Adult Theological Education*, Vol. 4.1, 2007.

Wraight, Heather (ed.), *UK Christian Handbook 2007/2008* (London: Christian Research, 2006).

Internet sources

www.timesonline.co.uk/tol/comment/faith/article2175753.ece

www.culf.org.uk/files/summary.pdf (accessed on 31 July 2007).

www.cpas.org.uk/growing/content/index.php (accessed on 8 August 2007).

www.worldwidelearn.com/online-degrees//index.html (accessed on 10 August 2007) .

www.resourcechurchplanting.com (accessed on 8 August 2007).

www.urbanexpressions.org.uk/crucible (accessed on 8 August 2007).

www.forge.org.au (accessed on 10 August 2007).

www.st-helens.org.uk/training_ministry/associate_scheme.php?e=135 (accessed on 31 July 2007).

Notes

1　Webber, R.E., *The Younger Evangelicals* (Grand Rapids, MI: Baker, 2002), 170. Webber uses the phrase to describe a new generation of evangelical distinct to the 'Billy Graham-esque' traditional evangelical or Bill Hybels' post-1970s pragmatic evangelicalism.
2　Gibbs, E., *LeadershipNext: Changing Leaders in a Changing Culture* (Downers Grove, IL: InterVarsity Press, 2005), 9.
3　McLaren, Brian D., *A New Kind of Christian: A Tale of Two Friends on a Spiritual Journey* (San Francisco, CA: Jossey-Bass, 2001), 145.
4　Gibbs, *LeadershipNext*, 9–10.
5　Cray, Graham, et al., *Mission-Shaped Church: Church Planting and Fresh Expressions of Church in a Changing Context* (London: Church House, 2004).
6　White, Heath, *Postmodernism 101: A First Course for the Curious Christian* (Grand Rapids, MI: Brazos, 2006), 14.
7　David is a composite personality characterized by many conversations with people who feel a strong sense of direction towards leadership in ministry and mission but who would avoid institutional ministry training at all costs.
8　Claiborne, S., *The Irresistible Revolution: Living as an Ordinary Radical* (Grand Rapids, MI: Zondervan, 2006), 14.

9   Jane is a composite personality characterized by involvement with a variety of people who respond well to more traditional and orthodox means of training and leadership.

10 Roxburgh, A.J., *The Sky is Falling: Leaders Lost in Transition* (Eagle, IL: ACI, 2005), 21.

11 Wraight, Heather (ed.), *UK Christian Handbook 2007/2008* (London: Christian Research, 2006), 420ff.

12 Banks, Robert, *Reenvisioning Theological Education: Exploring a Missional Alternative to Current Models* (Grand Rapids, MI: Eerdmans, 1999), 4.

13 Wilton, Gary, 'From ACCM22 to Hind via Athens and Berlin: A Critical Analysis of Key Documents Shaping Contemporary Church of England Theological Education with Reference to the Work of David Kelsey' in *Journal of Adult Theological Education*, Vol. 4.1, 2007, 31ff.

14 Gibbs, *LeadershipNext*, 198.

15 Webber, *Younger Evangelicals*, 171.

16 McLaren, *A New Kind of Christian*, 150.

17 Gibbs, Eddie and Ian Coffey, *ChurchNext: Quantum Changes in Christian Ministry* (Leicester: InterVarsity Press, 2001), 108.

18 McLaren, *A New Kind of Christian*, 150.

19 Grove, Daniel, in *The Baptist Times*, 7 June 2007, 1.

20 Gibbs, *LeadershipNext*, 200.

21 Little, Brenda, 'Higher Education and work-based learning' in *Higher Education Digest*, Summer 2007, Issue 58, 7.

22 Coffey and Gibbs, *ChurchNext*, 99.

23 See www.forge.org.au (accessed 10 August 2007).

24 See www.culf.org.uk/files/summary.pdf (accessed 31 July 2007).

25 As encouraged by the *Fresh Expressions* report of the Church of England and, for example, in training courses such as STETS in the South of England, SEITE in the South East and CBDTI in the North West of England.

26 Roberts, Michael, 'Thread in the Formation of Faithful Clergy' in *Contact: Practical Theology and Pastoral Care*, 152; Faithful Cities, 2007, p. 35.

27 Webber, *Young Evangelicals*, 163.

28 See www.st-helens.org.uk/training_ministry/associate_scheme.php?e=135 (accessed on 31 July 2007).

29 Roberts, *Faithful Clergy*, 35.

30 *New Frontier*, The Salvation Army College for Officer Training at Crestmont, USA Western Territory.

31 Coffey and Gibbs, *ChurchNext*, 114.

[32] Campolo, Tony, 'Missing the Point: Seminaries' in *Adventures in Missing the Point* (Grand Rapids, MI: Zondervan, 2003), 178.

[33] Miller, Donald, *Reinventing American Protestantism: Christianity in the New Millennium* (Berkeley, CA: University of California, 1997), 188.

[34] Cray, *Mission-Shaped Church,* 135.

[35] Cray, *Mission-Shaped Church,* 135.

[36] See www.cpas.org.uk/growing/content/index.php (accessed on 8 August 2007).

[37] See www.urbanexpressions.org.uk/crucible (accessed on 8 August 2007).

[38] See www.resourcechurchplanting.com (accessed on 8 August 2007).

[39] Charles-Maurice de Talleyrand, 1754–1838.

[40] Sandercock-Brown, G., 'Embrace the Tension', *Officer,* Jan/Feb 2006

[41] Roxburgh, *The Sky is Falling,* 21.

[42] Roxburgh, *The Sky is Falling,* 144.

[43] Roxburgh, *The Sky is Falling,* 157.

[44] Jamison, C., *Finding Sanctuary: Monastic Steps for Everyday Life* (Collegeville, MN: Liturgical Press, 2006), 121.

[45] Webber, *Young Evangelicals,* 166–9.

[46] Stephenson, P., J. Goode and C. Cole, 'I still haven't found what I'm looking for: Why do Generation X struggle to find a place in Mission Agencies' in Tiplady, R. (ed.), *Postmission: World Mission by a Postmodern Generation* (Carlisle: Paternoster, 2002), 14.

[47] Coffey and Gibbs, *ChurchNext,* 95.

[48] McLaren, Brian D., 'Missing the Point: Seminary' in *Adventures in Missing the Point* (Grand Rapids, MI: Zondervan, 2003), 180.

[49] McLaren, *Adventures in Missing the Pont,* 181–2.

5

The Call, Training and Leadership: Biblical Reflections

Derek Tidball

Just as global warming is reshaping the contours of the earth's surface, so we live in an exciting transition time when the contours of church and ministry are being reconfigured. Old institutional structures are failing and new forms of communal Christian expression are emerging. Yet, underneath the much-debated changes, certain issues prove of enduring significance for those who become leaders among God's people.[1] Effective servant leadership in the Church depends on four elements: call, charisma, competence and character. Each element is distinct from the others but not disconnected. All four overlapping factors keep recurring and are seen as essential in the unfolding narrative of scripture.

The call

From at least Victorian Britain on, until relatively recently, the standard model in evangelical churches concerning the call to ministry was that of the 'heroic' call. Applicants were advised not to enter ministry unless they had a definite sense of vocation. This consisted not only of an overwhelming inner conviction that this is how they should spend their lives but also, frequently, of some specific encounter with God in which his voice was heard issuing the invitation. The encounter with God might come through a sermon, in one's daily Bible reading, when one was alone praying or, quite often, at a special camp or Bible convention, possibly even in a crisis showdown with God. It was matched by the advice, often attributed to the Victorian Prince of Preachers, Charles H.

Spurgeon, that no one should enter the ministry if they could do anything else with their lives.[2]

The personal call alone was not considered sufficient. Various additional dimensions of the call were added: circumstantial (is one in a position to fulfil a call?); providential (has one got the gifts which matches the call?); and ecclesiastical (does the or at least a church confirm the call?). Some of these will be explored later.[3]

Such advice stood the test of time well. Ministry can be stressful and lonely and only those who were convinced that God had placed them there could persevere. But it may not have been altogether an honest understanding of the process[4] and wider changes in the Church and world called this 'heroic' concept into question. First, the world of work became peculiarly open in a way unprecedented in earlier generations. Before the Second World War few people had much real choice regarding their occupation and once they secured a job they remained in it until their long service was honoured by the presentation of a gold watch. Now the choices are legion and people frequently switch jobs not only mid-career but even every couple of years.

Second, there was a lowering of the sacred / secular divide and many Christians began to rediscover a more biblical doctrine of work which saw all Christians as called, whether they were clergy, accountants or dustmen.[5] This position had been advocated by Luther and Calvin in Reformation times but Protestants, no less than others, had tended to forget it since then (unless you had a vocation as a doctor or nurse!). The Keswick Convention, for example, which did so much to shape evangelicalism, reinforced in the popular mind the unbiblical view that the people who were really called were pastors and overseas missionaries. But, thankfully, this has been challenged in recent years.

Third, the winds that swept through the churches from 1960s onwards associated with the charismatic movement, dethroned not only the organist and his or her place in the music of the church, but in many cases, the minister and his or her place as exclusive preacher, leader and worship specialist in the church. The 'laity'[6] began to participate in worship much more actively raising questions about why one needed to be especially trained and ordained as a minister in order to function in church leadership. Did not Paul's image of the church as the body (1 Cor.

12) teach that all members of the church had an important gift to contribute, not just 'one man' standing at the front? Most recently some advocates of the 'Emerging Church' have championed the view that leadership should never be hierarchical, should be much more being alongside rather than over, and should even adopt the apostle, prophet, evangelist, pastor, and teacher model of Ephesians 4:12.[7]

So where does all this leave the idea of 'the call'? My first answer is this: these changes do not exempt those taking responsibility within the church from their need for a call from God, rather they strengthen it. The fact that others are called to serve God outside the institution of the Church does not mean that those who serve God within it do not need a call. The emphasis is that *all* are called, Christian leaders no less than schoolteachers or car mechanics. Furthermore the resurrection of the body imagery in worship highlights the idea that some are called to be prophets, pastors and teachers and they, like others in the church, need a call from God to contribute their gift constructively.

My second, and more significant, answer is to say that in any case scripture, not culture, needs to be our benchmark. It is apparent in the Bible that all major figures who played a part in leading the nation or the Church had some form of call experience. From Abraham in Genesis 12 to Timothy in 2 Timothy 1:6, a call is evident. Indeed, it is remarkable how even within the minor prophets, where their literature is often extremely brief, care is taken to begin with at least the formulaic statement, 'the word of the Lord came …', stressing their sense of commissioning.

However, any honest review of these calls must come to a two-fold conclusion. First the calls are extremely varied. Secondly, we do not know as much about them as we would like.

For some, like Moses, Isaiah, Jeremiah, Ezekiel or Paul, they take the form of dramatic encounters with God, often accompanied by visionary experiences. For others the call was mediated through other people, as in the call of King Saul or King David, who were both anointed by Samuel. In a different way, we read of Paul and Barnabas appointing elders in the churches that they had founded (Acts 14:23). For still others the call might be said to be more circumstantial, but no less real, as with Joshua, Moses' heir apparent, Deborah, Israel's judge called to lead in a crisis, or some of the early church leaders, like Stephanus and Nympha (1 Cor. 16:15–16; Col. 4:15), who hosted the church in their houses.[8]

Further honest reflection on the way God's call came to many biblical characters compels us to say how little rather than how much we know about the mechanisms of their call. Often we are simply told, 'The word of the Lord came', without further explanation. We may surmise what this means. Micah's calling, for example, because of the vocabulary used, was almost certainly through a vision. Indeed some Bible translations make this explicit. But in other cases it could have been a voice or just a strong sense-impression.

Given the evidence, it must be right to claim that some form of call is essential but, given the variety, it is also right that such a call should never be stereotyped and expected to conform to some neat pre-programmed package. God meets us where we are in ways that get through to us which will differ, not least, because we are different personalities. We dare not merely drift into Christian leadership today without any sense of call any more than it would have been right to do so in the past. To do so is to be presumptuous and that brings a host of ills in its wake. It leads to self-appointment rather than a God-appointment, in an area where pride is a constantly prowling enemy against which we should always be on our guard.[9] However much we may protest that ministry is about serving, ministry and leadership do confer status. They offer the possibility of exercising power and consequently the possibility of feeding our hunger for recognition and standing as a celebrity. A call from God tells us it is his ministry not ours. We are only obeying orders! Moreover, to enter ministry without a call is to risk the spiritual health of others. Just as we would not trust our physical health to self-appointed doctors who claim to know a lot about medicine but can provide no evidence that they do, so we should not trust the spiritual health of people who are not suitably commissioned (and qualified, but more of that later) to practice spiritual medicine. What is more, experience shows that although some have found self-appointment to lead to a wonderfully fulfilled egocentric life, even more who have sought to lead the Church without God's call have crashed out in disillusion and despair.

The core characteristics of any Christian call are found in that issued to the Apostles by Jesus, as it is recorded in Mark 3:13–14. Jesus chose 12 'that they might be with him and that he might send them out ...'. Here is the secret. The tension at the heart of effective ministry is the tension of intimacy with Jesus and involvement in the world. Staying close and going far are both involved in 'ministry'. There are twin distortions to be avoided. Some have wonderfully intimate relationships with Jesus but would be terrified ever to, as it were, leave his side and venture into his broken world; while others are so immersed in his broken world that they have lost touch with him who alone is the source of all healing and truth.

Walter Brueggemann has pointed out that the very idea of the call is profoundly counter-cultural today, since we seek autonomy, rather than being accountable to someone. His comment must be taken seriously.[10] We need to be sure that in revising our ideas of a call we are not in reality abandoning the idea of the call because we put personal choice or comfortable culture above the recurring example of Scripture.

Charisma

Calling is one thing, charisma another. By charisma I do not mean the charisma of the modern personality cult (perish the thought!) but the grace bestowed by the Holy Spirit so that the called person serves in a way that benefits the Church and gospel. Such charisma comes in two forms, one general and the other specific.

The first charisma necessary for effective leadership is a general filling of the Holy Spirit. Having the Holy Spirit living as a permanent resident within one's life is the essence of the Christian life. There can be no distinction between a belief in Jesus and receiving the Holy Spirit since the Spirit is none other than the Spirit of Jesus (Acts 2:38; Rom. 8:9). Yet the Spirit's residency is not to be taken for granted by believers. We need to take care to nurture it and ensure that his presence and work in us are unimpeded. Paul uses three images to stress this. First, there is the image of the army marching in formation when we are told to 'keep in step with the Spirit' (Gal. 5:25). Second, there is the image of maintaining friendships or relations when we are told not to 'grieve the Holy Spirit of God' (Eph. 4:30). Third, there is the image of fire fighting when we are warned not to put out the Spirit's fire (1 Thes. 5:19).[11] It is clear from these commands that although Christians possess the Spirit there is a careful work of maintenance to do in guarding the relationship by avoiding sin, by living obediently to Christ, by refusing to spurn his leading and by allowing him to transform us in holiness.

There are those who would gloss over this aspect of the Spirit's work in us in order to reach the more specific work of the Spirit through which he gives us particular gifts to equip us for ministry. But to do so is to try to run spiritually before we can walk. The sovereign God is quite capable of overcoming all our failings and lack of holiness and still using us. Samson is just one example of his doing so. But God's ability is no excuse for our inattentiveness to his plain requirements and should never be used as an excuse for spiritual indolence. His normal method of working is to use those who, though they are not perfect, are walking closely with him as his friends and subjects and are, in other words, 'filled with the Spirit'.

In addition to the general filling of the Spirit that is necessary for leaders, the Bible often highlights a particular connection between the gift of the Holy Spirit and a person's competence to undertake the tasks of leadership. The connection is mentioned from the earliest days of Israel's history. Moses and Joshua are equipped for leadership by the Spirit, but so too are the elders of Israel (Num. 11:16–29, 27:18). 'The Spirit of the Lord came on' the Judges, like Othniel and Gideon (Judg. 3:10 and 6:34). Kings were marked out by the Spirit (1 Sam. 10:5–7 and 16:13), and the hallmark of the prophet was the direction of the Spirit over their lives and words (see, e.g. Is. 42:1, 61:1–3; Mic. 3:8). The same connection between leadership and the Holy Spirit is evident in the early church. When, for example, they appointed seven leaders from among the Hellenistic believers to work alongside the apostles the Church was told to choose men who were 'known to be full of the Spirit and of wisdom' (Acts 6:3).[12]

The connection is equally evident when Paul speaks of leadership as a gift of God that should be exercised with diligence by those who have it (Rom. 12:8). While Paul's fuller teaching on the gifts of the Spirit do not explicitly mention the gifts of leadership, there are several gifts mentioned in 1 Corinthians 12 that are specific leadership gifts – such as the gift of the apostle, prophet and teacher, and even the gift of the 'pilot' variously translated into English as the gift of administration or of guiding, but in reality the gift of steering the Church.

1 Corinthians 12 sets out a number of crucial issues if we are to understand the sort of leaders God wants for his church. The opening verses clearly set the tone. They are people who, although they may have a natural talent for leadership, exercise something different that is not merely that. Those who exercise spiritual gifts use their abilities not for their own ends but for Christ and his church. They do so with an attitude of humility and, by adopting the role of the servant, they become a channel of God's grace to build others up in the faith.[13] Self doesn't come into it. Verses four through six tell us that what we call 'gifts of the Spirit' are, in actual fact, the gifts of the Trinity: the Spirit distributes them, the Son serves his church through them and the Father energizes its life by them. This means that although God may use natural talents in the Church he may equally sovereignly override them. It also tells us that if we are using natural talents of whatever kind we must be careful to ensure that they are daily consecrated to Christ and used for his glory and his alone.[14]

The major thrust of Paul's teaching regarding spiritual gifts is that they are distributed throughout the body of the Church, so none can claim omnicompetence. We need each other and are incomplete without each other. Consequently, no one has any claim to superiority. But equally, nor has anyone any claim to inferiority, for every member of the body of Christ is gifted in one respect or another and has a contribution to make to the whole. This calls into question some hierarchical views of leadership where the clergy are in practice viewed as having all the gifts, however much we may deny it in theory.

So, leaders will not only be those who walk in harmony with the Spirit but who have a particular gift from God which will render service to the Church; a particular endowment that gifts them for one aspect of leadership or another.

Competence

Again, the question of competence falls into two categories: the general and the particular. And again, what is said here needs to be qualified by recognizing the sovereign God is more than capable of overriding our lack of competence and using us to accomplish his will. Nonetheless, we work on the basis of what the Bible presents as the norm and should never use God's sovereignty as an excuse for our sloppiness or ineptitude.

General competence relates to a general ability to handle life. When Paul set out for Timothy the qualifications to be sought in elders, deacons and women leaders[15] he spoke of the former needing to 'have a good reputation with outsiders' and the latter being 'worthy of respect' (1 Tim. 3:7,8,11). His perspective is largely determined by the question of character, but this cannot be divorced from competence and it is obvious that he is looking for people who can manage their families, their finances and themselves well. In some respects Paul's teaching echoes that of Jesus when, in explaining the parable of the shrewd manager to his disciples (Lk. 16:10–12), he talks of the need to prove trustworthy in handling material things, even if they are trivial and belong to someone else, before being trusted to handle 'true riches'.

Some of this thinking lies behind the custom of ministerial selection conferences which expect candidates to have wider life experience before they present themselves for ministry. But the point is not quite the same. Merely having wider life experience may or may not prove useful. It depends what one learned from it and – and this is the point – how one has handled it. Sadly I have known a number of people over the years who have made a mess of their work life and look to the ministry as an escape route. I have equally known others who for different reasons – perhaps because of their inability to handle finances or their inability to command respect – would fail these general tests of competence and yet think the answer to their personal lack of success lies in leading the Church. Unfortunately, TV's caricature of the vicar as someone who is a spineless and ineffectual weed is not without some basis. According to the New Testament, it is a fair question, if people are presenting themselves for leadership, to ask what impression they have created as a neighbour, family member or employee.

In addition to the general question of competence there is the need to look for competence in the more specific areas of leadership to which one feels called. I do not believe that we should fragment Christian leadership too much into watertight compartments. A pastor also needs to be an evangelist (according to 1 Tim. 4:5), and an evangelist must accept responsibility for being at least an initial teacher of the faith, and a leader almost certainly will exercise their leadership through or in partnership with one of the other gifts and not just be 'a leader', and so on. Even so, we have probably not thought as sharply about this area as we should have done. If, for example, someone said to you they wanted to train for medicine, almost certainly you would want to know which branch of medicine they were talking about. Although there is a great deal of general expertise shared across the whole medical field, there is a difference between a GP and a surgeon, a radiographer and a nurse, a paediatrician and a vet, and the training is shaped appropriately. So it is in Christian service.

What particular gifts is a person seeking to exercise and what evidence is there of competence in that field? I have met people who claim to be evangelists but who have never led anyone to Christ, and indeed, in some cases only ever succeeded in alienating people from him! Pastors might be expected to handle people well. Teachers who leave their congregations confused might well have their calling as teachers called into question. Paul speaks of their need to be 'able to teach' (1 Tim. 3:2). Prophets whose prophecies prove false are warned in scripture of the serious consequences of being a false prophet. Leaders who only divide and ruin the Church have probably mistaken their gift.[16]

How, then, can we identify what gift we have? And what should we do about it when we have done so? Several factors come together in identifying a gift. Almost certainly there well be an inner conviction that this is how God will particularly use us, akin to the call, which we discussed earlier. But that on its own is not sufficient. The conviction is likely to prove a comfortable fit. It does not always do so and there is more than one example of a prophet like Jeremiah who never really came to terms with his call and ministered throughout his life uncomfortably. But the traditional view that if you want to do it, it cannot possibly be from God, because he calls us to suffering and sacrifice, is almost certainly untrue, at least when applied across the board. It makes God out to be an inefficient creator who merely displays his power by making round pegs fit into square holes. He knew us before we were born and was shaping us from our earliest moments. Paul is an outstanding example of the way God shapes and equips someone for the ministry they are going to fulfil from the start of their lives. Who else was better qualified to be an Apostle to the Gentiles on behalf of a Jewish Messiah in the Roman Empire than a Jewish Pharisee who had been educated in Tarsus and had the status of a Roman citizen? That sounds like the sort of thing God might well bring about.

To the call and the fit, we must add the evidence of success and the confirmation of others. If you believe you have the gift of an evangelist, ask yourself how many people you have won to be disciples of Jesus? If you have the gift of leadership, who's following? If you are a teacher, do people say, 'Ah, now I understand!'? Small steps can be taken in all these areas and then an objective assessment of the response can be made in order to build up a picture that confirms one's leading or suggests we're not thinking on the right lines. Then it is important to seek confirmation from others. Of course, some people will think it very unspiritual to do anything but encourage people who say they are called, even when they know they are not. So, in seeking confirmation, seek the guidance of an objective kind, like the guidance of older, wiser Christians, rather than just one's peers, or even one's mother. If this is done, people should be able to approach a selection committee with humble confidence.

But, say one has discovered one's gifts, what then? This is where training comes in. It is a very false antithesis to say that because one is gifted one need not train. Exactly the opposite is true. There is no point in training unless one is gifted and if one is gifted one has a responsibility to develop the gift to the full. In fact, as John Chrysostom – one of the great leaders of the early church – argued the greater the gift, the greater the responsibility to train it.[17]

Again, the New Testament evidence is clear. Jesus spent three years with his disciples (learners), including many off-the-road times in private, teaching them what they would need to know. Even then he couldn't teach them everything but it was a foundation on which the Holy Spirit would build (Jn. 16:12–13). He usually taught them in small groups rather than one-to-one: they were a community of learning. His instruction was sometimes very practical, such as teaching them how to evangelize (Lk. 10:1–24) or pray (Lk. 11:1–13). Sometimes it was instruction in character or leadership that he gave them. Sometimes it was pure theology he taught them (Jn. 13–16).[18]

When Paul was commissioned on the Damascus Road as the Apostle to the Gentiles, he did not rush into service but spent three years in the Arabian Desert and after that went up to Jerusalem to consult with the Apostles before beginning his preaching missions (Gal. 1:13–21). Timothy, the one whom Paul says was charismatically gifted through the laying on of hands (2 Tim. 1:6–7), is nonetheless instructed to be a worker who correctly handles God's word and to find approval from others (2 Tim. 2:15). Furthermore the element of training is implicit in the images Paul uses of Christian service, like that of the athlete (1 Cor. 9:24–27; 2 Tim. 2:5).

It has been fashionable recently to argue that even if the need for training is granted, the sort of training to be sought is that of 'apprenticeship training' or on-the-job training. But this is only partly true. Training in the early church was certainly training in skills and character but it was not thereby devoid of training in theology. We have seen how the disciples formed 'a community of learning'. Once the Church spread and leaders emerged from Gentile backgrounds who did not have the advantage of the foundations already laid in Jewish monotheism, other patterns and communities of learning began to emerge as a response to need.

In our age, there is still much room for apprenticeship-type training, but there are also some limitations to it. Its advantages are that it is skill-oriented, practical and demonstrates the 'how to' of the task in real – not textbook – terms. Its disadvantages are that it can be too focused, too narrow and sets before the learner one way of doing things. So it is great at reproducing younger models of the teacher. But it can leave many questions unanswered and often does not get behind the reason for the practice or provide training in skills that are transferable elsewhere.

The advantage of the Bible or Theological College is that it can and does instruct in a range of necessary disciplines in a concise and systematic way. So it does get behind the practice issues and answers some of the deeper questions. Although they vary, most Bible and Theological Colleges today are anything but ivory tower academies that answer remote questions no one is asking. Certainly in the college I lead my colleagues have a huge practical track record and continue to be highly engaged in the Church and the world or I wouldn't have appointed them. The questions we face today whether in the area of ethics, belief or apologetics, are complex – and what a wonderful opportunity is provided to engage in having one's thinking challenged and shaped in a concentrated way by others before we find ourselves pronouncing dogmatically on things we've never thought of from a platform or pulpit somewhere.

Colleges, too, are acutely alert to practical training and issues of character and spiritual formation. Many of them have mentoring schemes. Students are not removed from the world for several years and then sent back into it, but continue to engage all the time they are training. One of the good trends in recent Higher Education has been the emphasis on what outcome a diploma or degree course provides in terms of transferable skills and the type of person who graduates. This has been to our advantage in training people in theology that neither needs to be nor should be anything but exclusively an academic disciple.

Of course people can and do serve in Christian leadership without such training. The Spirit is able to equip in more than one way. But too often people claim the training of the Spirit when their work suggests they must have been absent when he was dishing it out. It has sometimes been claimed to justify ignorance and sloppiness which is not only spiritually dangerous but also does anything but glorify God. It has always seemed strange to me that people should question the value of training. We would not think of questioning the value of training in any other sphere. We would not be happy at flying in a plane with an untrained pilot at the controls, or permitting our body to undergo surgery at the hands of an unqualified doctor. So why do we think we can get away with less when it comes to serving the cause of Christ? Training of some sort is both a New Testament imperative and a contemporary necessity. Only so will any competence God has given us usually be developed to the full.

Character

The final area that is essential is that of character. This is where the greatest emphasis falls in the New Testament. We do not find an easy job description outlining what the minister or leader should do in the New Testament – partly because of the absence of the sort of ordained leadership we have become accustomed to and partly because the New Testament is not a book of systematic theology but a series of documents forged under the inspiration of the Spirit for the living church. But there are plenty of character descriptions to be found, especially in 2 Timothy and Titus. The New Testament is much more interested in the type of person who leads than the mechanics of leadership.

Taking 1 Timothy 3:1–7 as our template, we note that competence is referred to, as we have seen, (overseers must be 'able to teach', verse 2) but character is stressed above all. The list of qualities might be expressed something like this. Paul says leaders should be faithful in marriage, even in temperament, outgoing in hospitality, free from addictions (whether to violence, quarrelling, money or drink), respected by their children, exemplary in reputation, and mature in faith.

Most of these touch a contemporary raw nerve. We have grown accustomed to politicians and other public leaders excusing their behaviour as a purely private matter. But this can never be so in the church. The private and the public are inevitably all of a piece. So, we are called up to have high standards of family life and loyal to our wives (or husbands). Self-control is necessary in the areas of temper, as well as sex and money matters. Undoubtedly Paul would today add drugs and Internet pornography to his list of addictions from which we should be free. In a world of victims when so many are wrapped up in their own problems, the note he sounds about hospitality reminds us of how others rather than self should be the centre of attention. And the emphasis on maturity suggests we should know our way around the faith both in terms of belief and practice. For it to have been tested over time is no bad preparation for leadership. It needs to be robust to withstand the inevitable discouragements that will come with the territory.

Peter Kusmic has wisely said, 'Charisma without character is catastrophe'. Perfection is not required or else none of us would be able to lead; we are all flawed characters. But the basic standards and determination needs to be present. However gifted one might be, unless those gifts are housed in a stable character, the gifts might prove destructive rather than positive.

Contemporary culture is more concerned with personality, especially celebrity personality, than character. Personality has been defined as 'an ill-defined concept embracing the entire constellation of psychological characteristics that differentiate people from one another'.[19] It is about whether someone is extrovert or introvert, anxious by disposition or imperturbable. As David Wells says, when we speak of personality the adjectives that come to mind are 'fascinating, stunning, attractive, magnetic, glowing, dominant, forceful'.[20] But character is a moral quality, about good or bad, right and wrong, and the virtues, such as integrity, meekness, purity, speech, perseverance, and generosity. While the Bible is silent on the question of personality it is rich and expansive on the question of character.

The psychologists differ, but the consensus appears to be that it is difficult to change our personalities much. But character is a different matter. It can be nurtured, cultivated and trained, which is what Paul says when he tells Timothy, 'train yourself to be godly. For physical training is of some value, but godliness has value for all things' (1 Tim. 4:7,8). In saying this, Paul was assuming the ancient world's view that the training of the whole person was comparable to the training of the body for athletics.[21] Indeed, in Greek culture the training of the one was considered to have a great deal to do with the other. But, just as in athletic training, the competitor is stretched beyond their original limits through exercise, so the Christian leader can be stretched through reflecting deeply, and with others, on their experience. Experience alone is not enough since it is untrue that we automatically learn through experience. It's what we do with the experience that counts!

Much of our contemporary Christian culture has been seduced into believing the wider cultural view that personality, rather than character, is what matters. Some of our big and exciting events, which local churches often seek to replicate, have a role in feeding this. But the biblical ideal, held out as an aspiration for us all, is that leaders should be people who are trustworthy in character. Consequently, attention should be paid as much to this in the selection and nurturing of emerging leaders as to the gifts they offer.

In leadership, call, charisma, competence, and character belong together and if any one is missing then leadership will be at best the weaker for it and at worst fatally flawed. But when they exist, they can and should be developed to make us even better leaders in Christ's church, whatever shape that church takes.

Bibliography

Banks, Robert, *Paul's Idea of Community* (Exeter: Paternoster, 1980).

Bruce, A.B., *The Training of the Twelve* (Grand Rapids, MI: Kregal, 1971).

Brueggemann, Walter, *Hopeful Imagination* (Philadelphia, PA: Fortress, 1986).

Chrysostom, John, *On the Priesthood*, Book 5.5, Nicene and Post-Nicene Fathers, ed. Philip Schaff, Vol. 9 (Grand Rapids, MI: Eerdmans, 1889).

Clowney, Edmund, *Called to the Ministry* (Phillipsburg, NJ: Presbyterian and Reformed Publishing, 1976).

Colemen, Andrew, 'Personality' *The Social Science Encyclopaedia* ed. A. and J. Kuper (London: Routledge, 1996).

Davison Hunet, James, *The Death of Character*, (New York, NY: Basic, 2000).

Frost, Michael and Alan Hirsch, *The Shaping of Things to Come* (Peabody, MA: Hendrickson, 2003).

Gibbs, Eddie and Ryan Bolger, *Emerging Churches* (London: SPCK, 2006).

Griffiths, Michael, *The Example of Jesus* (London: Hodder & Stoughton, 1985).

Guinness, Os, *The Call* (Nashville, TN: Word, 1998).

Kimball, Dan, *The Emerging Church* (Grand Rapids, MI: Zondervan, 2003).

Niebuhr, H.R., *The Purpose of the Church and Its Ministry* (New York, NY: Harper & Bros, 1956).

Spurgeon, C.H., *Lectures to My Students* (London: Passmore & Alibaster, 1900).

Tower, R., and A. Coxon, *The Fate of the Anglican Clergy* (London: Macmillan, 1979).

Turner, Max, 'Holy Spirit' in *New Dictionary of Biblical Theology* (Leicester: InterVarsity Press, 2000).

Wells, David, *Losing Our Virtue* (Leicester: InterVarsity Press, 1998).

Wilkey Collinson, Sylvia, *Making Disciples: The Significance of Jesus' Educational Methods for Today's Church* (Carlisle: Paternoster, 2004).

Notes

[1] I will mostly use the term 'leader' or 'Christian leader' throughout this paper in a deliberate attempt to be inclusive and recognize that leadership in the contemporary church does not lie exclusively with the ordained ministry.

[2] Spurgeon endorses this advice in *Lectures to My Students* (London: Passmore & Alibaster, 1900) 23, but attributes the remark to an unnamed wise divine.

[3] H.R. Niebuhr gives classic expression to these in *The Purpose of the Church and Its Ministry* (New York, NY: Harper & Bros, 1956). Another variation is found in Clowney, Edmund, *Called to the Ministry* (Presbyterian and Reformed Publishing, 1976).

[4] Sociologists, for example, can interpret people's call to ministry purely in the terms normally used for the recruitment process in other professions. This highlights the human factors involved in the call in contrast to the divine element. See, for example, Tower, R., and A. Coxon, *The Fate of the Anglican Clergy* (London: Macmillan, 1979). It also led some candidates for ministry distorting their real experience so as to express it in terms that bishops, elders and other church leaders would want to hear.

[5] One of the most thoughtful discussions of this is found in Guinness, Os, *The Call* (Nashville, TN: Word, 1998). He distinguishes between our primary calling as disciples of Christ to live and do everything in a way that honours God from our secondary calling to an occupation. He rightly protests that simply equating our call with our work is a 'Protestant distortion' of Biblical teaching. The call is much wider.

[6] This author believes that it is impossible to sustain a view of the clergy/laity distinction from the New Testament, even if some people are set apart from particular leadership roles and functions within the church.

7 See, for example, Frost, Michael and Alan Hirsch, *The Shaping of Things to Come* (Peabody, MA: Hendrickson, 2003). Wider reflections, especially contrasting leadership in the Emerging Church with the CEO model, can be found in Gibbs, Eddie and Ryan Bolger, *Emerging Churches* (London: SPCK, 2006), 190–205 and Kimball, Dan, *The Emerging Church* (Grand Rapids, MI: Zondervan, 2003), 227–41.

8 On this see Banks, Robert, *Paul's Idea of Community* (Exeter: Paternoster, 1980).

9 This is the reason why Paul insists in 1 Timothy 3:6 that young believers should not be recognized as leaders too soon.

10 Brueggemann, Walter, *Hopeful Imagination* (Philadelphia, PA: Fortress, 1986), 19.

11 The RSV puts it starkly: 'Do not quench the Spirit.'

12 For an excellent summary article of the development of the doctrine of the Holy Spirit in the Bible see, Turner, Max, 'Holy Spirit' in *New Dictionary of Biblical Theology* (Leicester: InterVarsity Press, 2000), 551–8.

13 Paul, of course, did not invent this emphasis on servanthood. See what Jesus says in Mark 10:42–45.

14 The implication of this is that although there may be much to learn from secular leadership we must be careful never to adopt ideas uncritically and must always transpose any teaching into a key that harmonizes with the New Testament's teaching on leadership.

15 The reference to women in 1 Timothy 3:11 is unclear. It might refer to deacons' wives but may also be a reference to senior women who exercised leadership in the church.

16 This is no theoretical argument. I can unfortunately give more than one illustration of every example mentioned here.

17 'For though the preacher may have great ability (and this one would only find in a few), not even in this case is he released from perpetual toil. For since preaching does not come by nature, but by study, suppose a man reach a high standard of it, this will then forsake him if he does not cultivate his power by constant application and exercise. So there is greater labour for the wiser than for the unlearned.' Chrysostom, John, *On the Priesthood*, Book 5.5, Nicene and Post-Nicene Fathers, ed. Philip Schaff, Vol. 9 (Grand Rapids, MI: Eerdmans, 1889), 71ff.

18 Those who wish to pursue Jesus' education of his disciples are referred to Bruce, A.B., *The Training of the Twelve* (Grand Rapids, MI: Kregal, 1971); Griffiths, Michael, *The Example of Jesus* (London: Hodder & Stoughton, 1985); and, most recently and especially, Wilkey

Collinson, Sylvia, *Making Disciples: The Significance of Jesus' Educational Methods for Today's Church* (Carlisle: Paternoster, 2004).

[19] Colemen, Andrew, 'Personality' in *The Social Science Encyclopaedia* ed. A. and J. Kuper (London: Routledge, 1996) 599.

[20] Wells, David, *Losing our Virtue* (Leicester: InterVarsity Press, 1998), 97.

[21] For an interesting discussion of the recent position see James Davison Hunet, *The Death of Character* (New York, NY: Basic, 2000).

6

What Can the Church Learn about Leadership, from the World of Business

Peter Holmes

Introduction

Although some of us may like to think that the Church is 'unchangeable', society as a whole, and newcomers to church life in particular, will continue to challenge such ideas and practices. Each generation must review what is important for the future, e.g. the fundamentals, and what can be left behind. This process we are beginning to call 'Ancient Future Church' is now underway. This ongoing review of the processes and practice of faith, together with its theological framework, needs to be explored and lived for both our and future generations.

One such area now under heavy review is the Church's models of leadership. Successful ideas and their leadership practice have stood for hundreds of years. Congregational and even denominational life has largely been shaped by the Church's ideas and practices regarding leadership. But any organization reflects both the strengths and weaknesses of those that lead it. This 'traditional' approach to leadership we now call the 'top down' approach. One person leads, while all the committees, groups and everyone else follows. Despite its numerous flaws, this model in one form or another has served the wider Church well for hundreds of years. So why should we change now? Contemporary society is suggesting why.

Postmodernism

Elsewhere in this book the reasons for this review of how we lead the Church becomes obvious. The collapse in numbers of new candidates entering traditional Christian ministry is now a deep cause for concern, as are the standards and competence of this dwindling intake. But as society rapidly changes, faith communities are being forced to re-think their outlook and practices. 'Change or die' are some of the watchwords, so many faith communities have died.

Society's postmodern ideas and values have left many Christians upset and confused. Society's live-and-let-live attitude, the belief that religion is trouble, the attitude that Christianity is a spent force, and a range of other such ideas are now all taking their toll. Christianity is no longer the dominant religion. Pluralism, the idea that 'all faiths lead to God, don't they?', alongside the live-and-let-live 'broad mindedness' of people today, all leave Christianity as just one of the faiths to choose from. Christianity is no longer the power it once was. So many young people today, within postmodernism, have an instinct to abandon what some of their parents continue to value in the Church. While valuing Christ they feel less of a duty toward traditional church.

As a result 'postmodern Christians' largely perceive much Christian training as time-warped, stuck in the dark ages, irrelevant to the street pastor or youth worker of today. In some ways, sadly, this could be true. For instance, the Church since the birth of psychology and its therapies in the 1800s seems to have been left behind, now vainly trying to catch up with a society and culture that has long since declared itself well able to care for itself without religion. Nowhere is this stark separation more obvious than in the world of business. Here many Christian ideas, like work ethic, self-worth and the concept of spirituality have all been passionately embraced, but nowadays without the encumbrance of religion. But other ideas in postmodernity are not so obvious, for instance the concept of holism.

The rise of holism

One of the key values of postmodernism has been the rise of holism or, as some call it, wholism.[1] This is the simple idea that society, even the whole world, is a closed system.[2] Everything that we do impacts everything else. We now know that there is no such thing as a discrete (e.g. private, enclosed) act for any of us. For instance, in the field of personal health we are moving from a place where we have traditionally treated the disease, to a place where we now treat the person as a whole. Along similar lines, we now know it is better to buy an apple grown locally than one with a carbon footprint from Colombia. Such holistic thinking is now beginning to re-shape the world that we live in. It is driven by commercialism.

But aspects of holism are also impacting us in numerous other ways. Goleman among others is helping lead this charge. In 1995 he published '*Emotional Intelligence*'. This book sets the stage for the now fashionable rise of a healthy view of emotion and its application.[3] EQ is now seen as an essential asset in management and leadership. As a result we are witnessing the birth of a whole new field of research and thinking.[4] Go to any business exhibition and note the numerous EQ consultants! Sceptical Graeco-Roman ideas about human emotion are giving way to a more balanced holistic view of our feelings. We are now beginning to learn that we need our feelings more than our IQ, if we are to lead successfully. EQ is part of a wider picture that now presents itself.

But in 2006 Goleman did it again, opening a further field of holistic thought. This time he offered us *Social Intelligence*. In this book he suggests that human nature is created (e.g. intentionally hard wired) for empathic relationship. The solitary Cartesian male is now dead, as is the flawed distinction between nature and nurture. They cannot be distinct, because we are one whole as people. However most of this holistic thought is happening outside the Church,[5] even though the view that human nature should see emotion as an asset is also consistent with Hebrew thought, while the concept that people are created for empathic community is consistent with the idea of social Trinity.

Therefore, in any thinking about leadership in the Church it is important to bear in mind that 'godless' society actually has lots of wisdom for the Church. Some is denied within the Church (e.g. that emotion and its feelings are an ally), while some has been forgotten (e.g. the Cappadocian social Trinity). So in this article I will suggest that concepts like holism, EQ and social intelligence are all ideas the Church could usefully learn from, were it willing. So what can we learn from contemporary ideas of leadership outside the Church, and from the social and economic climate within which much of this is evolving?

Leadership today

The subject of leadership has in some ways been the holy grail of business, and the subject of an enormous quantity of popular and academic literature. Although in this article we are only confining ourselves to leadership in business, even this is a vast and growing field, with thousands of books being published every year. Though if we are to teach the Church about leadership it could also learn much from other fields like academia, government, education, and even politics.

The background

Most organizations today would acknowledge the problem of achieving an appropriate balance between top-down, bottom-up and lateral processes of leadership and management.[6] This is made even more complicated within many organizations by internal struggles at inter-departmental levels, and with the additional conflict between line functions (e.g. authority, budgetary control, etc.) and staff functions (e.g. managing, serving). Also, with the rapid changes in commercial life many organizations are being forced to 'rationalize', that is, shed staff, re-organize, and 'flatten'. By flatten I mean the levelling of traditional hierarchies so there are fewer people involved, and more direct access, e.g. an 'open door' between directors and staff at all levels. New thinking in leadership has been needed to help facilitate such significant positive change. Let us landscape recent thinking in leadership in business.

Leadership today must precipitate positive change

All leadership today, one way or the other, is about positive change (see Susan Williams' article, pp. 111–29). That is, change is needed in both the systems and the individuals in it. But first we need to better understand both the structural dimensions of an organization and also the human resource aspects. When these are both better understood we can then set about changing both in a positive way. Leadership, to effect such positive change must always understand and embrace both structural and human dimensions of an organization.

But the emphasis on holism also reminds us that all structures, due to the human factor, are always dynamic and changing. To insist on remaining the same, in a commercial sense, is to court suicide. But because of postmodern ideas like holism organizational structures are no longer perceived as static. Though in moving toward a model of positive change we must be careful not to return changed individuals into unchanged systems, or vice versa, like we are sometimes doing with our newly trained young Christian leaders. The whole climate of postmodern society is a cauldron of change, so positive change is fundamental to modern ideas of leadership, and in turn raises questions of the leadership style needed for such organizations.

Leadership styles

Numerous books have been written about leadership styles, with the view now being adopted that one needs to develop a range of skills that allow you to adjust your leadership style to accommodate the specific needs of situation or people. It is no longer acceptable to press your style on everyone just because it is your way of doing the job. In this sense we are moving toward more bespoke leadership styles that are less directive, more holistic and far more adaptive to need. But organizations, especially institutions, like individuals, also need to adapt and change in positive ways. This phenomenon we are now calling 'learning organizations'.

Learning organizations

All organizations in postmodern society, in order to survive and prosper, must become 'learning organizations'. They must remain on the cutting edge of change and its technology, continually evolving as an organization. Such ideas help bring alive the organic nature of organizations, whereby all its assets and property are seen as 'capital', that must be both added to and adapted, as society and its needs also change. Behind such thinking is a profoundly simple idea, that it is not always of merit to strive to remain the same.

Not only must one change, but as an organization one must also be able to build capital into both structures and into personnel. So learning is about survival and prosperity, the capacity to adapt and prosper by what one is learning. Not unlike the human body, which every seven years or so has completely replaced all its living cells, while remaining much the same. Likewise, leaders are no longer just leaders, but have a range of differing duties, including being learners themselves.

The benefit of distributed leadership

In business leadership we are moving from a place where managers need some training, to a place where leadership training has been considered essential, but now toward leadership that is 'distributed'. That is, that every person at every level is expected to be a leader in one-way or another. By 'distributed' I mean the devolvement of both the authority and responsibility of leadership from one person at the top, to delegated responsibility and power at lower and even all levels. One of the features of post-modernism is the emphasis on the responsibility of the individual for themselves, rather than being merely a 'cog in a big machine'. We are moving from the age-old reflex of blaming the boss, or the 'stupid management' for the plight the company is in, to a place where everyone is expected to get involved. So everyone needs to keep learning at all levels of the organization.

Business as a life-long learning journey

Leadership has itself also become a learning journey, not any longer a single qualification or label we earn, then once we've got it, we forget. Instead, in best practice all staff in an organization have personal development plans, learning goals that are specifically agreed with them. This may lead to further qualifications, or attendance at training days, or the regular reading of certain trade journals.[7]

The increasing value of 'soft skills'

Because of the rise of EQ emotional qualities of leadership are more highly valued today, e.g. being considerate, fair, having integrity, trustworthy, a participator, good communicator, credible, positive, competent and able to think through matters. These 'soft' skills mean one is more interactive, participative and experiential. Mentoring, coaching, active learning, job shadowing, role play, self study, and personal reflection are just some of the training aspects of this. Emotion, and the learned skill of coaching it, is now on the agenda.

One of the most highly prized soft skills is the ability to manage difficult situations well – building trust, initiating reconciliation and opening up dialogue. This is the art of dealing with difficult people, managing conflict, and having the ability to read the signs of what is really going on both in and between people. Such soft skills are today most normally learned from mentors or by coaching, rather than in the classroom.

The power of mentoring and coaching

A significant growth area in leadership in business is the idea of leaders mentoring or coaching learners. A substantial literature is emerging with a range of emphases from preparing people for top management to offering 'tasters' of what it is like to be a leader. It is an emerging field all of its own. One aspect of this is 'succession planning', identifying and training leaders for the future.

The need for inspirational leadership

There is a growing demand for inspirational leadership in all sectors of society. By this we mean leaders' ability to encourage and release others' potential. Numerous writers are picking up this theme. But along with being inspirational, leadership must also be ethical,[8] and morally based. Most of the basic qualities valued in a leader today are ethically upright. Only through such leadership that is trusted are we able to build successful commercial communities.

Building commercial communities

Personal identity today seems integrally linked to motivation and experience of leadership, as suggested by Sergiovanni, who identifies five key characteristics for sustainable leadership, creating learning communities that are collegial (mutual gain), caring, inclusive (mutually honouring), and inquiring in nature (collective enquiry). This in turn brings us to one of the most significant shifts in contemporary management, the concept of building teams.

The move towards team models

The twenty-first century is seeing the rapid rise of the collaborative teams. In business, as part of this shift, there is a significant move away from traditional management hierarchies, toward collaborative leadership. People are joining together to build teams. We have already noted the growing interest in whole organizations learning, the increased value of soft skills, and the need to build enterprise around commercial communities. But we have also noted the increased interest in collective or 'distributive' leadership that in itself devolves into greater strategic and operational autonomy for middle and lower management.

Integration, embeddedness and collective engagement are today increasingly central to the effectiveness of leadership, especially in sectors like Higher Education. Society is placing greater value on informal networks and relationships. We are moving away from Cartesian thinking, where everyone can happily exist on their own isolated islands.

Some of the reasons behind this shift are the continuing concerns in society regarding the issue of power. Through the media the abuse of power is daily in our faces, forcing increasing numbers of people to ask questions regarding the wisdom of leaving power in the hands of a few. One response to this is the attractiveness of devolved leadership models. But as this increases, with power normally devolving downwards, it then raises questions about what to do with the disempowered senior staff?

Business is therefore beginning to see the need for balance. We should not be over-reacting by seeking an either/or option of hierarchy or teams. Instead we should be seeking more symbiotic models that combine best practice from both contemporary and more traditional models in building teams. Some are already beginning to call this 'blended leadership'. Such a move means that teams are continuing to be attractive for a number of reasons, and are increasingly finding their place in business. Let us look at some of the features of these teams.

Group IQ

Society is moving toward what the government calls a 'knowledge economy'. By this we mean either the value and economy of knowledge, or the evolving knowledge-based economy. Put simply, knowledge is increasingly valued in the marketplace because we are moving from a manufacturing based economy, where vocational skills are valued, to a knowledge economy where intellectual ability is most valued. With the increasing sophistication of society and business the need for a wider knowledge and skill base is becoming essential for success. Knowledge is increasingly seen as currency.

One of the reasons for this is that we are moving toward a global economy. You make a local call and talk to a call centre in India, or get on the web looking for a second-hand tool box, and locate the ideal one, but it turns out to be it Hinton, Iowa, USA. With this 'global village' effect comes the need for both different and increased levels of skill. Even servicing a car is no longer about plugs and oil filters alone, but lap-tops, databases, relays and management systems. It is becoming increasingly important to understand the narrative fabric of organizational life, if one is to compete and excel.

So success in business increasingly needs both a cluster of skills in oneself, but also a team of people who are all uniquely skilled and willing to contribute their own skills toward the benefit of the whole. One no longer needs twenty bricklayers, but five people on a team, all of whom bring a range of diverse and unique skills.

Mixing and matching individual skills is more important today than having batches of the same vocational skill. Put another way, business is beginning to admit, in its own commercial fashion, that we need one another in a way we have not in the past. Teams are important, but made up of people who all contribute in their own unique way. Together they make up a group IQ that must be ever learning and continuing to change and grow. But this IQ must also stand alongside what is now being called social capital.

Social capital

By social capital, I am talking about a person's location within a network of relationships. In a business sense it is the investment in social relations, in turn yielding a range of profitable returns in the marketplace. What the theory of social capital suggests is that people with the biggest or most effective networks are those that succeed, while those without them fail. Successful business is about being in the right place at the right time with the right product and network. As a result many businesses today are moving into social action, seeking to be more 'green', and encouraging their staff to 'get involved' in what are perceived to be positive interventions in society.

But social capital also includes looking within themselves as an organization for more social opportunities. Most people have latent ideas of making money, or inventing products, or improving services in the organization. Many people have in the past worked in a business for many years, watching the daily incompetence and waste of both time and resources. Today, with its greater social awareness, many top management teams welcome the airing of new ideas, and the possibility of implementing such ideas. Some of the simplest can be highly profitable, like printing all copies double-sided, adopting flexi-time, hot-desking (sharing a desk), and compensating staff for positive performance.

The implications of such thinking are profound, forcing people to look at their own 'cabbage patch' existence, and their resistance to committing to business and relationships. But with this move to joined-up social capital, more and more people are living alone, with an alarming rise in social autism, together with increased 'selfism'.[9]

So while these point to a breakdown of social capital, we are also seeing in business the creation of a greater need for networking and building lasting relationships. Teams teach us all how to do relationships more effectively. As in numerous other areas business is leading the way, encouraging staff at all levels to become more actively involved in both business and society. One of the outcomes of this is what is now being called 'shared social identity'.

Shared social identity

By shared social identity we are talking about a megatrend in society toward the need for people to work together for the common good, to be part of a team. Embracing a shared social identity is increasingly seen as essential for both leadership and business success today. The admission is that none of us can do it alone. Shared social identity is also essential for successful communication and workgroup activity.

What we are learning is the power of shared identity. Being part of a successful group like Jobs Apple Team, or Branson's Virgin empire gives to all of us something we need: a reason to commit. What we are noting is the simple principle of synergy, where one plus one equals five. But such thinking also bucks the trend toward social isolation, by giving us good reasons to commit. From such books as Goleman's *Social Intelligence* we are learning that what we can accomplish together is far more than we can ever do alone. But other aspects of shared social identity are also of interest to us.

The success of common purpose and goals means we are able to tackle matters and issues that we cannot when alone. Building teams for specific tasks is a key aspect of contemporary business life today, whether it be the project management of moving British Airways into terminal five at Heathrow, or finding alternative energy sources for an isolated manufacturing plant. The cohesion of social identity allows us to move ahead when it would be too dangerous or formidable alone.

At its best having a social identity also gives us something as individuals. It can help build our personal identity. Belonging is one of our deepest human needs, and when we do not belong we are lost. Our self-worth is profoundly undermined. So it is important that we all belong somewhere. The business world is very aware of this, and is doing much to build social networks within organizations, whether it is the badminton team, life coaching or meditation classes at lunchtime. Teams build and feed on what they give to its members. But such thinking then moves us on into shared responsibility.

Shared responsibility

One of the greatest attractions in building teams is that one is able to share responsibility with others. By this I mean that no one person has all the power and *all* the responsibility. Responsibility is shared by everyone, and therefore more manageable. Also, because everyone brings a range of unique skills, as a team one is more able to adapt to changing markets, demands and circumstances.

But sharing responsibility also allows newcomers to both see and learn how to do this for themselves. What they need to learn in joining a team is that every one of us is reluctant to carry responsibility when it comes with accountability, and few of us really learn this skill well. But if we are willing to do so it will, in turn, spawn a whole range of benefits to us – such as wanting to learn more, maybe pursue professional qualifications, learn more about where our natural skill sets rest – and the ability to adapt our developing leadership skills to new challenges.

The business world has more to teach us when it comes to responsibility: we are compensated (hopefully well, much of the time!). In being recognized for our commitment and skills we are able to move on and up, so that we also find in this process of carrying responsibility the pleasure of compensation. The need to be recognized and affirmed for what you do well is essential to personal wellbeing. Every one of us needs to know we are loved and valued. But the rise of interest in teams has also raised a whole host of problems for many of us, related to questions of gender.

The gender issue

In business life today changing commercial needs, best practice and legislation, among other factors, have all contributed to the rise and greater value of women in the marketplace. But women still only represent two per cent of board members worldwide, while very few women are among the wealthiest people. For instance, only three names appear in the top 30 on the UK Rich List, and even these tend to share the slot with either husbands or partners.

One of the numerous postmodern ideas is that gender equality should be seen in every area of society. So women are now moving in large numbers into fields like medicine, banking and other service industries. On the whole they are being welcomed, because most of these are growth areas and many prefer women at lower and middle management positions. Greater female EQ skills and a willingness to work in teams are, as we are noting, more highly valued today. In many ways the twenty-first century will be the century of women. So where do all of these ideas leave us here in the Church?

Drawing some of these ideas into congregational life

It is no accident that business's increasing emphasis on quality leadership is also taking up a range of biblical themes. For instance Neuschel looks at servanthood as a model of leadership, while Jones looks at the leadership model of Christ himself. Again, Woolf draws out from Scripture the leadership model of men like Moses and Matthew. Ethical leadership is another area, as is the idea that leaders should be people of integrity, honesty and have an ordered personal life .

Along similar lines there is now a biblical attractiveness in the team model (e.g. disciples and support groups, etc.), together with the one-to-one discipling of others (e.g. mentoring or coaching). Many of these biblical themes and their practice are now coming of age in society. But society is leaving one thing out: religion. While speaking of ethical leadership, for instance, one conveniently forgets where this ethic comes from, e.g. Scripture and the fruit of the Spirit.

What will be becoming obvious to you as you read this brief article is that we are looking at something of a circular process. The church has in the past been the depositary of such thinking regarding leadership in society. There are very few new ideas. But the borrowing of so many of these ideas by the business world has in turn divested it of the encumbrance of bad, toxic or arrogant religion, making it something we can all usefully learn from. Daily in my business and professional life I hear all manner of ideas and principles being enthusiastically talked about, and with ease they relate back to Scripture and the church's traditions. Let us now summarize some of these.

Positive change, holism and building communities as learning organizations

Western Christianity has in some ways forgotten that we all need to change to be like Christ.[10] Also, we seem to have overlooked the fact that Scripture does not glory that much in the solitary saint. Instead, church is about building communities, about constantly changing and about being a learning organization. Christ comes to us when we are together (Mt. 18:20). What seems to have happened is that many of these traditional Christian values have not been sustained in contemporary Western congregational life, so we are now looking at business and society as a whole needing to remind us in the church that very often these are Christian. But this is not the case with the issue of leadership and leadership styles.

Leadership styles, inspirational leadership and distributed leadership

Churches, through traditional training, tend toward one main way of preparing its leaders for service: theological college. It is because of this that we are writing this collection. So today, unfortunately, in some ways we are still holding on to a stereotypical leader in the church. College-trained in theology, with a professional or business background, and a clear idea of what leadership is about, based mainly on what we have ourselves experienced.

What society is now saying to the Church is that leadership is not a style or type, but requires a range of skills that requires the leader to change their style of leadership depending on their changing circumstances. Each new challenge brings change in the leader themselves so they are able to meet the needs of both the circumstances and team members' changing circumstances. Within a church setting this will mean they are able to adapt as and when this is needed. But throughout they are inspirational and able to delegate in ways that honour the members. Training in such skills will require a range of EG, SQ and IQ training based on practitioner models, rather than lecture theatre taught. But other skills must also be learned.

Integrity, soft skills and managing conflict, mentoring and coaching

Society, like business, is (re)turning to values that are traditionally presumed to be part of church life, but today without the religion. These include the ability to calm a tide of anger, skills in discipling, learning the power of a soft word, and inspiring the virtues of Christ-likeness. But what is different in business are the values placed on the reasons why we must live this way. In business, for instance, the 'Investors in People' programme or the return of the apprenticeship is valued because it is good business, not because we have been commanded to do so, as in the church.

But a number of other distinctions also exist between business and the church. In business best practice is purposely taught so that it can easily be measured, whether from the bottom line or the atmosphere in the office. In contrast, in local congregational life we have few ways of measuring success, apart from numbers on a Sunday or the collection plate.

In the church new ways need to be found for measuring positive change and its values, in order to draw out best practice. Much of this will need practical hands-on training as opposed to cognitive, cerebral thinking, becoming more a group responsibility than that of any one individual. For instance, forgiveness and laying down revenge are timeless teaching in the church, but how do you teach these at a practical clinical level? This needs to become the work of whole communities.

Team models, group IQ, social capital, and shared social identity and responsibility

This area should be the greatest embarrassment to the Church. Teams, group IQ, social capital and identity are seminal to both Scripture and traditions in the Church. But where today does one find these being valued and lived out in local church life? Since the Enlightenment especially, the pyramid hierarchy of leadership and the 'professionally' trained practitioner have now become the norm. Presbyterial ministry and sacrament have in some ways prevailed, for good and for bad. Also, following Cartesian attitudes there has been a shift away from community or corporate thinking to the importance of the one, and the rise of selfism.

In business focus on teams has become more and more fashionable over the last 20 to 30 years, though in some ways now waning in favour of a balance between teams and more traditional hierarchies. Mixed in with this is the gender issue, where women are today more welcome in both the boardroom and in management. But women should also be allowed to lead by their strengths, not merely be expected to 'compete' with men on male terms.[11]

A work in progress

What does seem obvious is that the Church will need to begin to show greater grace and humility in being willing to recover much that it has forgotten, while also seeking to learn from both business and society. The jury is presently out on whether the Church, as we now know it, will or can learn these important lessons.

Bibliography

Adair, J., *The Inspirational Leader: How to Motivate, Encourage and Achieve Success* (London: Kogan Page, 2004).

Bavister, S. and A. Vickers, *Be Your Best Coach … and Beyond* (London: Q Learning, 2003).

Blanchard, K. and D. Shula, *The Little Book of Coaching: Motivating People to Be Winners* (London: HarperCollins, 2002).

Bolden, R., et al., *Developing Collective Leadership in Higher Education: Final report for the Leadership Foundation for Higher Education* (Exeter: University of Exeter, 2007).

Coxon, I., 'The Sunday Times Rich List', *Sunday Times* (29 April 2007).

Fiske, S.T., *Social Beings: A Core Motives Approach to Social Psychology* (London: John Wiley, 2004).

Fullan, M., *The Moral Imperative of School Leadership* (Ontario: Corwin Press, 2003).

Gerhardt, S., *Why Love Matters: How Affection Shapes a Baby's Brain* (London: Routledge, 2004).

Goleman, D., *Emotional Intelligence* (New York: Bantam Books, 1995).

—, *The New Leaders: Transforming the Art of Leadership into the Science of Results* (London: Little Brown, 2002).

—, *Social Intelligence: The New Science of Human Relationship* (London: Hutchinson, 2006).

Greener, R., *48 Laws of Power* (London: Profile Books, 2002).

Hamm, R.L., *Recreating the Church: Leadership for the Post-modern Age* (London: Chalice Press, 2007).

Holmes, P.R., *Trinity in Human Community: Exploring Congregational Life in the Image of the Social Trinity* (Milton Keynes: Paternoster, 2006).

—, 'Spirituality: some disciplinary perspectives' in Flanagan, K. and P.C. Jupp (eds.), *The Sociology of Spirituality* (London: Ashgate, 2007).

Holmes, P.R. and S.B. Williams, *Becoming More Like Christ: Introducing a Biblical Contemporary Journey* (Milton Keynes: Paternoster, 2007).

—, *Emotion: A Biblical Handbook. Feeling is Healing* (Denver, CO: Authentic Media, forthcoming).

Hunt, S. and P. Hutcheson, *Leadership for Women in the Church* (Grand Rapids, MI: Zondervan, 1991).

Jaworski, J., *Synchronicity: The Inner Path of Leadership* (San Francisco, CA: Berrett-Koehler Publishers, 1998).

Jeffers, S., *Feel the Fear and Do It Anyway* (London: Vermillion, 2007).

Jones, L.B., *Jesus, CEO: Using Ancient Hebrew Wisdom for Visionary Leadership* (New York: Hyperion, 1995).

Kottler, J.P., *Leading Change* (Boston, MA: Harvard Business School, 1996).

Kottler, J.P. and D.S. Cohen, *The Heart of Change: Real Life Stories of How People Change their Organization* (Boston, MA: Harvard Business School, 2002).

Leitch, S., *Leitch Review of Skills* (London: HM Treasury, 2006).

Leithwood, K., et al., *Challenging Leadership for Changing Times* (Buckingham: Open University, 1999).

Lovelock, J.E., *Gaia: A New Look at Life on Earth* (Oxford: Oxford University Press, 1979/87).

Maxwell, J.C., *Developing the Leader Within You* (Nashville, TN: Thomas Nelson, 1993).

Mintzberg, H., *Managers not MBAs: A Hard Look at the Soft Practice of Managing* (New York: Pearson Education, 2004).

Nan, L., *Social Capital: A Theory of Social Structure and Action* (New York: Cambridge University Press, 2001).

Neuschel, R.P., *The Servant Leader: Unleashing the Power of Your People* (Evanston, IL: North West University Press, 2004).

Niedenthal, P.M., et al., *The Psychology of Emotion: Interpersonal, Experiential and Cognitive Approaches* (Hove: Psychology Press, 2006).

Secretan, L., *Inspire: What Great Leaders Do* (London: John Wiley, 2005).

Senge, P.M., *The Fifth Discipline: The Art and Practice of the Learning Organization* (London: Random House, 2006).

Sergiovanni, T.J., *Building Community in Schools* (San Francisco, CA: Jossey-Bass, 1994).

Swabb, R.I., et al., *Small Group Productivity: Communication, Interpersonal Attraction and Group Identification* (Paper presented at the annual meeting of the International Communication Association, New Orleans Sheraton, New Orleans. Online <PDF>.2008-10-10 http://www.allacademic.com/meta/p113163index.html).

Woolf, L., *The Bible and Leadership: From Moses to Matthew, Management Lessons for Contemporary Leaders* (London: Amacom, 2002).

Notes

1. See http://en.wikipedia.org/wiki/Holism.
2. J.E. Lovelock, *Gaia: A New Look at Life on Earth* (Oxford: Oxford University Press, 1979/87).
3. Note, for instance, S. Gerhardt, *Why Love Matters: How Affection Shapes a Baby's Brain* (London: Routledge, 2004) or P.M. Niedenthal, et al., *The Psychology of Emotion: Interpersonal, Experiential and Cognitive Approaches* (Hove: Psychology Press, 2006).
4. See www.eiconsortium.org/.
5. For instance, S.T. Fiske, *Social Beings: A Core Motives Approach to Social Psychology* (London: John Wiley, 2004) devoted an entire book

to the idea of people being social beings, focusing on belonging, understanding, controlling, enhancing self, and trusting.

[6] For simplicity I am restricting myself to concepts surrounding leadership, but a book could easily be written about best practice in the field of management, and how the Church might learn from the latest thinking in this area as well.

[7] Space does not permit us to look in any detail at the growing number of 'self-help' books focusing on leadership. See for instance J.C. Maxwell, *Developing the Leader Within You* (Nashville, TN: Thomas Nelson, 1993) and J. Jaworski, *Synchronicity: The Inner Path of Leadership* (San Francisco, CA: Berrett-Koehler Publishers, 1998).

[8] Not everything that is taught is ethical! For instance, R. Greener's *48 Laws of Power* (London: Profile Books, 2002) talks about 48 laws for gaining power: Law 3 purposely conceals intention, Law 11 says you should learn how to keep people dependent on you, and Law 33 reveals how you can discover each man's thumbscrew (weaknesses), and (15) crush your enemy totally!

[9] P.R. Holmes, *Trinity in Human Community: Exploring congregational life in the image of the social Trinity* (Milton Keynes: Paternoster, 2006).

[10] Holmes, P.R. and S.B. Williams, *Becoming More Like Christ: Introducing a Biblical Contemporary Journey* (Milton Keynes: Paternoster, 2007).

[11] See http://www.futurechurch.org/wicl/index.htm.

7

Fit for Purpose?
Equipping the Church for the
Twenty-first Century

Susan Williams

It is perhaps self-evident to suggest that twenty-first-century churches are likely to be very different from their predecessors. The pace of change in society is so fast that even congregations with extensive treasured traditions in a denominational structure will find the local communities they serve are changing rapidly. New expressions of local church are also appearing. They may be niche churches, cell churches or parachurch groups, etc. Flory summarized Gen X religion as experiential and authentic, entrepreneurial, inclusive and that which offers identity in community.[1] Perhaps even this will change as GenXers approach retirement in 20–30 years time. And of course we still wait to see what GenY religion will look like.

Designing training programmes for those who will lead churches through these changes is therefore a significant challenge. What skills and competences will church leaders need? What knowledge and understanding will be essential for those called to full-time service? Should theological and academic training be a prerequisite for tomorrow's leaders? How important are a broad range of life skills, or the capacity for and commitment to lifelong learning? What is the place of character formation and a journey of growing Christ-likeness?[2]

These are complex questions, focused around the needs of the Body of Christ in the twenty-first century. But in most universities these days, when designing a learning programme the issues to be addressed are more commercially driven. Educators are asked to focus on the market demand created by learners. What combination of topics will generate interest? How will the course guarantee financial viability? What specialty can be offered by the mix of physical and human resources in the institution? It is the needs and priorities of the educational institution and qualifications authorities, rather than those of the Church, that drive the design of these types of programmes.

Denominations, independent Bible Schools and Christian training programmes may have more freedom to look ahead and anticipate the needs of the Church over the next 30–50 years. But as in so many areas of life, familiarity with the tried and tested approaches can often hinder more radical innovative thinking. So how can we build training programmes to support the development of leaders who can take responsibility for inspiring and leading the twenty-first-century church? What qualities do those leaders need, if the Church is to have a significant voice in twenty-first-century society?

It seems to me that designing training for future Christian leaders must take account of all these questions and many more beside. I have found myself asking, where would we begin, were we to have the freedom to start again, and design church leadership training that is *fit for purpose*? No doubt some of what is currently on offer would be included, but would there be other types of courses, other emphases and other options? What if we were to allow the best of academic, professional and vocational training to inform our strategy?

These questions are all the more timely because of the decline in regular church attendance in the West. The character of congregations is changing. Some congregations are facing an ageing process in pace with the age of existing members, with relatively few younger people. Others are having to adjust to a larger fringe membership, or greater networking through websites, chatrooms and other virtual expressions of community. These trends will create significantly different expectations of leadership compared even with those of the 1980s.

In this article I want to explore the possibility of a radically different model of leadership training for the Church. I hope it may contribute to a dialogue exploring innovative solutions to some of the challenges we are facing. I have avoided focusing on the more familiar academic and theoretical perspectives. Instead I have chosen to adopt the perspective of the training consultant and practitioner that I am, alongside my academic career.

Before considering a variety of ideas for twenty-first-century training, there are two contextual frameworks to explore that are highly relevant for our discussion. First, I will use the changing UK context of education and training to highlight the choices we face concerning forms of learning.[3] Then I will mention some ancient models of training that can offer a refreshing alternative to more recent traditions.

Knowledge, understanding and skill

While theories of learning abound, at a practical level the bulk of education in the UK has traditionally fallen into two categories, academic knowledge and vocational skill.

Academic study, usually university-based, focuses on the acquisition of cognitive *knowledge*, e.g. biblical studies, church history, apologetics, Greek and Hebrew. Academic training is particularly suited to the development of knowledge. This is something the Church has been expert in for hundreds of years.

Skill represents the other end of the educational spectrum. It refers to a capability in an activity, whether generic (e.g. team leadership) or specific (e.g. leading worship). It is typically developed as a more vocational qualification. Those who have significant skill will not necessarily have commensurate knowledge. Likewise those who have significant knowledge may not be able to demonstrate associated skill. I believe that for us to develop a practitioner model of leadership in the Church, we must seek to combine both academic competence and practitioner skills.

If knowledge and skill are viewed as a continuum, then in between them sits *understanding*. Conventionally understanding refers to the application of knowledge in context. For example, how do theoretical frameworks of pastoral care apply in the day-to-day context of local church life? Similarly it takes understanding as well as knowledge to take principles of church-planting and make them work effectively in cross-cultural settings.

In the British educational context recognition of skill has definitely played second fiddle to the recognition of knowledge. Those who know and have the capacity to 'think' have been esteemed more highly than those whose gifting and capacities are more focused towards what they 'do'. Vocational expertise has remained the poor step-sister of educational provision. It was assumed to be relevant for those who were unable to succeed academically, rather than as a field of expertise in its own right. By contrast, in Germany for example, a master craftsman with knowledge and skill, such as a clockmaker, is esteemed just as highly in society as a professor. Both are specialists, although one has expressed their expertise practically and the other intellectually. In the UK however, an expert in the trades is generally regarded as inferior to someone whose expertise is in knowledge.

This imbalance is about to be rectified. We are on the verge of a potentially radical shake-up in the provision of education and training. In 2006 Lord Leitch published his final report from his *Review of Skills* in the UK.[4] One of his findings is that much education simply does not equip learners with the skills they need for employment. The dichotomy between theory and practice seems to be creating a substantial skills deficit, leaving Britain falling behind other nations in international comparisons of qualification profiles.

If his principles and recommendations are adopted, training programmes and much educational provision will become increasingly employer-led. Rather than leaving the initiative with educational providers to design programmes that they expect to be of interest to learners, employers will be encouraged to participate in the approval of course content via sector skills councils. Development of skills specifically relevant for employers is becoming a prime objective in government policy.

If this development were to be adopted within the Church, local congregations, denominations and parachurch organizations would be given the opportunity to become the driving force behind training for members and leaders. With this new emphasis those on the ground in local churches could be invited to identify the knowledge, understanding and skill that their leaders need. Educators and trainers would then be called upon to provide appropriately accredited training programmes to meet those needs.

In anticipation of the adoption of the recommendations of the Leitch Report, I wonder what training programmes for Christian leadership might look like, if we were to undertake our own skills review? If local church members were to take responsibility for prioritizing the capabilities of their leadership, what would they want to focus on? What blend, for example, of theology, social intelligence and personal Christ-likeness? If being a lover of people was to be compared with understanding church history, which would be more significant for the church member? Perhaps it is unfair to present these topics in a polarized way, but it does help to clarify the choices we face and the changes we can consider making. Training in leadership and marketing, in interpersonal skill and emotional intelligence – or in chairing meetings, social psychology or the sociology of belonging – any of these might find their way into a new curriculum. Some may be academic, but perhaps an equal blend of understanding and skill development would be added.

When learning meant personal transformation

To a Christian leader of the Early Church, the legacy from the twentieth-century separation of knowledge, skill and personal attributes would look somewhat strange. In the ancient world, learning was a far more integrated and holistic exercise. This was not a world dominated by individualistic Cartesian thinking. Learning involved every area of one's personhood and relationships. And it always involved the requirement of personal positive change.

Hadot offers us some useful insight.[5] Philosophy, the core curriculum for those who would pursue learning, was primarily 'a way of life'. Those who had such learning had undergone a 'conversion' that led to a radical change in the direction of their life. As well as thoughts and beliefs, their perceptions of the world around them were fundamentally changed. This was accompanied by a lived morality, a transformed lifestyle developed as part of their learning. The goal of ancient philosophy was 'to form people and to transform souls'.[6] 'Spiritual disciplines' helped to provide opportunities for the 'practice' essential to ensure transformation occurred.[7] He suggests all six major philosophies of the ancient world followed these models.

Likewise, Christian monasticism was intended to produce a transformed life. Rather than the scholars, who lived their learning in the midst of the people, the monastics and mystics of the Early and Medieval Church withdrew to communities devoted to getting closer to God and building Christ-centred fellowships. This included extensive learning, which was expected to bring about personal change intended to impact every area of a person's life. Bruder's brief sociological study of monastic life gives an insight into this process at work in a community in the 1990s.[8] The intellectual, the application, the acquisition of skills, character development – they all blend indistinguishably in a journey of personal growth. The learning produced by such transformation continues to be a source of inspiration to many, even in our twenty-first century.[9]

In the Early Church there is some evidence that similar patterns of transformative change were expected of all new believers, even if not accompanied by scholarly study. Field, for example, suggests that catechumenates spent an extended period of time going through introductory discipleship programmes that included training in the faith, exorcism and learning Kingdom values.[10] They graduated after around three years and were baptized into the communion of faith. Leaders in the Early Church would no doubt have been trained in these processes and we can surmise that many would themselves have experienced them.

These models of learning therefore incorporated lifestyle change, growth of character, identity development, and changed relationships with others and with God. Those who were 'learned' were marked out by the quality of their personal life, their citizenship, their morality as well as their intellectual knowledge. Before the advent of universities, churches and monasteries were a primary source of such transformative learning.[11]

With Aquinas however, this pattern of learning began to change. The first university offered the opportunity for academic study that focused more exclusively on intellectual development. Here it became possible for students to specialize in academic learning, but without the rigor of the spiritual disciplines, or the responsibility of personal positive change. The gaining of knowledge and the power it gave became pre-eminent. Lifestyle, character and skill were no longer expected to develop alongside cognitive knowledge. Accreditation was individualized, emphasizing the rational. Integrity, relational competence and emotional development, for example, were no longer required for accredited learning.

The resulting chasm between the intellectual and the moral, the individualistic and the relational has often been noted. In his development of virtue ethics MacIntyre calls for the recovery of a moral philosophy, a real life morality that can offer an alternative to the over-emphasis on reasoning.[12] He proposes that such moral philosophy is an essential foundation for the sustaining of communities. Rooted in a non-reductionist view of self, such perspectives invite 'each human being [to] transform himself' to engage in a 'common effort, a community of research, mutual assistance and spiritual support'.[13]

In a similar vein there are a growing number of calls today for learning programmes that are transformative, for the development of 'learning power', values-based education and for integrated personal development planning. One of the opportunities facing the Church, if we were to redesign training for church leadership in the twenty-first century, would be to proactively create holistic programmes re-embedding personal transformation into learning.

Twenty-first-century leaders: the breadth of the problem

Before considering what such a holistic programme of training might be comprised of, our next task would be to consider who it is for. In designing leadership training programmes to equip the Church for her next 50 years (or until the Lord returns!), one possibility is that we consider adopting a broad understanding of leadership. The man or woman who knows they are called to a life of full-time service in the Church is one type of leader. But there are potentially many others. Perhaps we should be able to give opportunity for a wider range of people to take up the challenge, responsibility and privilege of leadership. Who are our potential new leaders?

With our changing demographics it is reasonable to assume that there will be many more who want to take up leadership roles in churches later in life. Some may be graduates and professional people. Others will have brought up families, or be experts in their trade and vocation. These will be people with extensive life experience, both good and not-so-good. Some may have pre-existing theological understanding based on years of church experience. Others will perhaps have little church background. We should not assume that all will be able to study full-time, nor even that all will be able to write 3,000-word assignments. Should this exclude them from leadership training?

Traditionally the emphasis in the Church has been on those who intend to take up church leadership as a life-long calling. And yet there will be some who may want to acquire church leadership training without committing to a long-term career in the Church. Perhaps these will have already demonstrated leadership capability in diverse contexts, and will want to integrate their skills with church leadership training and accreditation, prior to deciding their calling. Can these callings be significant *and* short-term?

When speaking of Christian leadership most people will instinctively think of a pastor or minister with responsibility for a church. But imagine the local church I am a part of, which had 10–20 men and women working together as a voluntary team, sharing responsibilities according to their natural and spiritual gifting and the ongoing needs of the faith community. Many had family and career commitments to integrate with their leadership responsibilities. Training was invaluable, sometimes as a team, and sometimes each bringing unique expertise.

Likewise, we must be aware of those churches with specialist ministries, perhaps international mission, or local mental health care, or a national worship or youth ministry. Or think of the cell church, where leaders of individual cells carry a diverse range of responsibilities for a small group. In addition to a core combination of knowledge, understanding and skill these churches have additional requirements of their leaders, based on the need and calling of the congregation.

Then of course there is the gifted and anointed man or woman who already knows that church leadership is a calling that they expect to follow for the rest of their life. They want to prepare for a lifelong ministry with a solid foundation of training. They would flourish within the kind of training programmes currently available in universities and bible colleges.

With such an extensive range of potential leaders how can a training programme be designed that will meet these needs? Their educational backgrounds will be highly varied. Many will have experienced some form of abuse in their history that will have created emotional weaknesses or perhaps even emotional illness. Some will have exceptional and proven gifting, but perhaps only in one specific area. Some will want training for their own pastoral context, perhaps *in situ*, rather than planning to serve another congregation. Some will expect a salary on completion whilst others will be able to support themselves through other means.

To equip such a range of leaders is indeed a challenge. What training will they want? What training will their churches want them to have? What are the attributes of a new generation of leaders that denominations will want to nurture. Will they be willing to admit weakness? Rather than recruiting the few, local churches seem to be welcoming many of these people into positions of leadership at a local level. They need training providers and educators to take a quantum leap to offer relevant innovative programmes. This new leadership will need to discover the ongoing personal transformation and learning essential for their unique callings.

Characteristics of new training programmes

Thinking outside the box – starting with the ideal – is a luxury that most of us cannot afford. We have budgets, institutional expectations, pre-existing syllabuses accepted by awarding bodies and denominational ordination processes. Yet it is the suggestion of this book that the time has come to take up a new vision and begin to radically rethink training for Christian leadership. So what might it include? The following are some of the characteristics that might be incorporated, if the goal were to offer a holistic leadership training programme to the many.

The model of Christ with his disciples

When Christ undertook leadership training He spurned those who considered themselves learned. Instead He started with a handful of men and their relational networks, who grew in their personal commitment to learn from Him. It was similar to an apprenticeship model, learning from a master in a way that required an integrated personal development including knowledge and skill but challenging their most personal of value systems and requiring a growing capacity to love. He seems to have expected everything about them to change as part of their discipleship journey. Provoking personal positive change is a core part of enabling Christ-likeness.[14]

Learner-centred flexibility

Postmodern people will bring with them their own expectations for learning programmes. They will question the relevance of certain modules for their own professional development. They will expect to be able to pursue their own interests and develop their own skills.

In the past, choice has often been restricted to a limited selection of optional courses or essay titles. However changes in qualifications frameworks are likely to create the opportunity for a much wider range of subjects and accreditation formats within one qualification. Will church-related training programmes be able to take a lead in providing such a breadth of opportunities? There are few contexts in which such a diverse range of people could take up leadership responsibility. Can we be proactive in tackling such a challenge?

Local church relevance

Borrowing from human resource management, it would be an interesting exercise for local churches to identify the 'person specification' of the various leadership roles in their own congregation. What range of skills, understanding and knowledge would be required? What passions, values and priorities should they bring? Do they see a pastor as a manager of an organization, such as a small business? If so, perhaps several units from a management qualification would be relevant. Alternately as so much of a minister's role is people-centred, perhaps human resource training would help, training in resolving conflict, leading teams, chairing meetings? Knowledge of organizational development, inspirational leadership or transformative change could be highly relevant to day-to-day responsibilities. In a world where employer-led training initiatives could become best practice, local churches can perhaps begin to identify their own requirements and shape the training they need for their leaders.

A growing Christ-likeness

As we have seen, alongside philosophy, theology is one of the oldest fields of learning. It has a rich legacy, where from the earliest biblical times character development and capacity for sustained relationship were intricately interwoven in the development of knowledge and skill. One of the tragedies of the Enlightenment has been the prioritizing of knowledge acquisition over personal development, so that it is now possible, at its most extreme, to be a university professor one day and, without dissonance to commit genocide the next.[15] Think of the child abuse scandals that have affected church leadership in recent headlines. Likewise the stories of manipulative leadership styles and abusive church environments point to an unhelpful disjuncture between knowledge and character formation in theological training.[16]

Society expects ethically consistent behaviour from its professionals. But as representatives of Christ the requirements of church leaders are even more onerous. What elements of a training programme equip an aspiring leader to provide a living example of growing Christ-likeness? Wholeness and personal development would seem to be core ingredients in any training programme for such leadership responsibility.

In the world but not of it

In a post-Christian age, day-to-day life for many church members involves living in Christ while engaging with a wider society that has little awareness of Christian values. The Body of Christ will need leaders able to tackle these challenges head-on, with wisdom and maturity, capable of winning the respect of their local communities. Who will offer support in matters of bullying, debt management, office politics, or domestic violence? What about local politics, school governance, interfaith dialogue or support for the retired? For the Church to remain a relevant voice, its members need to participate in such ventures. But this will require a breadth of leadership skill (and availability) that seems beyond the reach of many of our training programmes.

Innovative forms of accreditation?

Building a new vision for leadership training is a worthy initiative. But will it be sufficient simply to pour such new wine into old wineskins? My suspicion is that a transformative model of training for church leadership suitable for a highly-diversified pool of potential leaders will also require a radically different approach to both delivery of training and to accreditation. Let us start by considering the possibility of a more flexible accreditation framework.

I would suggest the ideas expressed in this paper so far require a person-centred approach to accreditation. One-size-fits-all simply will not work. If we are to value prior learning and expertise, both practical and intellectual, we must be able to cross-map relevant elements of previous qualifications. A holistic transformative learning programme will have units which accredit personal development and skill in addition to the acquisition of knowledge. How might this be favourably achieved?

The first task would be to ask what knowledge, understanding and/or skill would need to be demonstrated for a qualification to be awarded. This is more of a challenge than first appears. What learning outcomes might bridge the chasm that is often created by the polarity between academic and vocational frameworks.

Let us imagine a group of learning outcomes that have been compiled by an awarding body offering a postgraduate diploma in Christian leadership. Perhaps they have been proposed by local churches and parachurch organizations. They might include character development, emotional intelligence and social intelligence, as well as familiarity with theology and church history. Perhaps there will be optional modules offering a choice between, say, cross-cultural environments, pastoral ministry, or leadership of worship, or teaching or youth ministry.

A number of these would not best be accredited through written essays. Character development might be assessed through reflective logs and autoethnographic accounts. Cross-cultural ministry might be assessed through an extended report from a stay in an unfamiliar environment, whether overseas or simply a different neighbourhood. Pastoral ministry could be assessed through extended case studies.

Moving away from written accounts assessment might include observation reports from qualified assessors who have visited the learner and seen them demonstrate competence *in situ*. The experienced assessor will have an extensive repertoire of forms of evidence the learner can provide in order to demonstrate they have achieved the required competence. Witness statements from independent laypeople and clergy can provide additional evidence. Participation in moderated virtual environments or role plays, for example, can generate audit trails for assessment and accreditation. Perhaps each student will have responsibility for compiling a portfolio that reflects modules appropriate to their own ministry.

Moving to a portfolio of evidence as a basis for assessment offers a greater flexibility for the wide variety of people who might want to take up training for Christian leadership. It would allow the inclusion of essays and exams for some units of the qualification. But it would also provide for a creative expression of portfolio evidence to match the experience and competence of the learner.

Such portfolios of evidence would be particularly helpful for those entering Christian leadership training later in life. They would be able to draw from what is often a wealth of experience and competence in other leadership environments as a way of demonstrating their pre-existing skills. This would allow prior learning to be properly accredited, ensuring the learner is aware of how deeply their professional skills from other contexts are valued.

Flexible accreditation systems are of course quite challenging to administer. How can an awarding body ensure that the quality of their qualification is maintained? How can costs be managed when each learner portfolio is unique and when some modules require a number of assessed observations and discussions? The good news is that the Church will not need to reinvent the wheel. Vocational trainers have developed extensive experience in quality assurance and enhancement in on-site assessment, accreditation of prior learning, observation, etc. Other disciplines such as narrative enquiry and psychotherapy have practices suitable for the accreditation of autoethnography, counselling supervision, etc. When appropriately qualified and experienced trainers are used and when quality systems are in place, there is a wide range of accreditation options suitable for innovative training packages.

As a final consideration perhaps the most significant accreditation question is in the area of character formation and spiritual maturity. Put bluntly, should Christ-likeness and spiritual formation be accredited? The capacity to pursue one's own discipleship journey is surely a prerequisite for Christian leaders who will be expected to inspire and equip others to do the same. And yet while many church leadership training programmes expect personal and group devotional life to form part of the student experience, they frequently remain separate from the assessed curriculum.

Should spiritual maturity be assessed? Should the emphasis perhaps be on the journey of spiritual formation? Outside the Church there is a significant amount being written on spiritual health, its key dimensions and how it can be measured.

Innovative models of training

The idea I am exploring could consist of nationally (and inter-nationally) recognized qualifications designed to accredit potential leaders of churches and ministries. It could include elements tailored to fit the needs of a variety of local church and parachurch groups. It could be rooted in a non-reductionist perspective on self that integrates personal change and growing Christ-likeness with relevant knowledge and skill. It could even range from a Level 2 through to Level 7, allowing each learner to enter at an applicable point. It could be extended to incorporate continual professional development and opportunity for progression in a manner suitable to an individual's own ministry.

Once again we must be mindful of the diversity of learners who would benefit from a programme such as this. Without compromising the quality of training, however, there are numerous options for cost-effective delivery of training of such a modular portfolio-based award.

Underlying any model of training is a series of assumptions about who the learner is. Who are the recipients of such leadership training? Throughout this article I have assumed that there are many in positions of leadership in local churches. They are often small group leaders, youth leaders or worship leaders. They may provide leadership to a finance team, a welcome team or a refreshment team. With extra training in leadership skills these very committed volunteers will grow in capacity, grow in understanding and provide a rich resource for the pastor or minister to rely on. They may also find themselves with an opportunity to take up wider leadership responsibilities in due course. The Leitch Report recommends that a target of 40 per cent of the adult population should be qualified to Level 4 and above.[17] What target might we want to set for proportions of church members trained in aspects of church leadership?

I wonder if these kinds of approach to leadership training will help address some of the current weaknesses noted by other contributors to this book. They move away from the exclusivity of the pastor and spread expertise more widely throughout a congregation. Of course for those who want to focus on a long-term career in the Church there will still be academic degrees and ordination training programmes. But if other courses can be treated with equal respect and given appropriate endorsements within denominations and be widely available they might offer an excellent leadership training programme for a wider range of individuals.

One of the primary questions to be addressed is location. Training can be delivered within a university, college or campus context. But if more people are to be involved in such training it will become cost-effective to take programmes direct to a local church or group of churches. Then again the virtual world of the internet offers accessibility for those with home commitments, or those who find travel an obstacle. Perhaps there is no substitute for the opportunity to leave the apparent comfort of one's home environment and live closely with a number of strangers for an extended period of intensive training. But likewise training 10–20 members of the same church in spiritual formation and character development creates an invaluable opportunity for a sustainable network of relationships that can facilitate ongoing transformation.

Imagine a local church with a youth group who are keen to grow in leadership skill in Christian contexts at the same time as pursuing their own GCSE and A Level programmes. Their church could arrange a trainer to deliver a Level 2 training package over a series of one-day workshops, giving them an award in Christian discipleship. Perhaps this could be open to young people from other local churches, increasing financial viability whilst also building interchurch dialogue. When effectively delivered this entry level qualification would create interest in progressing to Level 3 and beyond, perhaps even building an expectation of lifelong learning in Christian discipleship and leadership. This could even be incorporated into an apprenticeship scheme perhaps at a regional or diocesan level or within a group of churches.[18]

Alternately imagine the man or woman facing 20–30 years of active retirement after a successful professional or trade-based career. With several short courses of accredited training their years of experience might be channelled into recognized leadership positions that offer a calling and purpose for what could be perhaps the most fruitful season of their life.

Conclusion

The Leitch Report is proposing that training is increasingly demand-led. If the Church were to begin to take this proposal seriously, it could create a quiet revolution in church leadership training. Those of us who provide training would go back to the members of local churches to ask them what types of training programmes they would like to have available, and what competences they would like their full-time leadership to have. The responsibility of training providers would be to then create modules and delivery systems that meet the needs of local churches in a cost-effective way.

This proposal would perhaps require a radical rethink of denominational and university training programmes. But if something similar to this were to be the preferred form of training to create a leadership ready to take the Church into her next 50 years, then surely now is the time to begin. Should we be thinking about an institute? Should we be actively contributing to the voluntary sector's discussions about a sector skills council?[19] Should we be raising up regional teams to train, accredit and disseminate best practice?

It seems absolutely essential that future curricula for Christian leaders must focus not around academic achievement but character development toward greater Christlikeness, a growing capacity to love God, His people and the world He has created. Let us mobilize an army of leadership, equipping them to let go of the emotional damage of their past, so that they can take their place in supporting and equipping the Body of Christ. If we cannot do this, then there is the very real risk that the Church will cease to be a force in a world that is valuing these things more and more.

The possibilities are endless. The consequences could be eternal.

Bibliography

Bruder, K.A., 'Monastic blessings: Deconstructing and reconstructing the self', *Symbolic Interaction* 21 (1998), 1. 87–116.

Field, A., *From Darkness to Light: How One Became a Christian in the Early Church* (Ben Lomond, CA: Conciliar Press, 1978/1997).

Flory, R.W., 'Toward a theory of Generation X religion' in Flory, R.W. and D.E. Miller (eds.), *Gen X Religion* (New York: Routledge, 2000).

Hadot, P., *Philosophy as a Way of Life: Spiritual Exercises from Socrates to Foucault* (Oxford; New York: Blackwell, 1995).

Holmes, P.R. and S.B. Williams, *Becoming More Like Christ: Introducing a Biblical Contemporary Journey* (Milton Keynes: Paternoster, 2007).

—, *Church as a Safe Place: A handbook. Confronting, Resolving and Minimising Abuse in the Church* (Bletchley: Authentic, 2008).

John of the Cross, *The Collected Works*, translated by K. Kavanaugh and O. Rodriguez (Washington: Institute of Carmelite Studies, 1979).

Kolini, E.M. and P.R. Holmes, *Christ Walks Where Evil Reigned: Responding to the Rwandan Genocide – Writing a Social Theology in a Rwandan Setting* (Denver, CO: Paternoster, 2008).

Leitch, S., *Leitch Review of Skills* (London: HM Treasury, 2006).

MacIntyre, A., *After Virtue* (London: Duckworth, 1981/1985).

Puhl, L.J., *The Spiritual Exercises of St Ignatius* (Bangalor: St Pauls, 1997).

Teresa of Avila, *The Interior Castle or the Mansions* (London: SCM Press, 1958).

Notes

[1] Flory, R.W., 'Toward a theory of Generation X religion' in R.W. Flory and D.E. Miller (eds.), *Gen X Religion* (New York: Routledge, 2000).

[2] Holmes, P.R., and S.B. Williams, *Becoming More Like Christ: Introducing a Biblical Contemporary Journey* (Milton Keynes: Paternoster, 2007).

[3] I have used the UK as a context for this article. However the principles can be extended into a wide variety of other national educational frameworks.

[4] Leitch, S., *Leitch Review of Skills* (London: HM Treasury, 2006).

[5] Hadot, P., *Philosophy as a Way of Life: Spiritual Exercises from Socrates to Foucault* (Oxford and New York: Blackwell, 1995).

[6] Hadot, *Philosophy*, p. 20.

[7] See, for example, Puhl, L.J., *The Spiritual Exercises of St Ignatius* (Bangalor: St Pauls, 1997).

[8] Bruder, K.A., 'Monastic blessings: Deconstructing and reconstructing the self', *Symbolic Interaction* 21 (1998), 1. 87–116.

[9] See, for example, Teresa of Avila, *The Interior Castle or the Mansions* (London: SCM Press, 1958); John of the Cross, *The Collected Works*, (Washington: Institute of Carmelite Studies, 1979).

[10] Field, A., *From Darkness to Light: How One Became a Christian in the Early Church* (Ben Lomond, CA: Conciliar Press, 1978/1997).

11 I do not wish to romanticize these environments. There is no doubt that some were also corrupt and did not help develop personal Christ-likeness.

12 MacIntyre, A., *After Virtue* (London: Duckworth, 1981/1985).

13 Hadot, *Philosophy*, 274–5.

14 Holmes and Williams, *Becoming More Like Christ*.

15 This was the tragic experience of some in Rwanda during the 1994 genocide. For more information, see Kolini, E.M. and P.R. Holmes, *Christ Walks Where Evil Reigned: Responding to the Rwandan Genocide – Writing a Social Theology in a Rwandan Setting* (Denver, Colorado: Paternoster, 2008).

16 Holmes, P.R. and S.B. Williams, *Church as a Safe Place: A handbook. Confronting, resolving and minimising abuse in the Church* (Bletchley: Authentic, 2008).

17 Level 2 is often characterized by 5 GCSEs at grade A to C but also various vocational qualifications; Level 3 is seen as the equivalent of 2 A Levels; Level 4 is often characterized by both university degrees as well as some professional qualifications e.g. in teaching and nursing.

18 See for example the government's Apprenticeship Blueprint at http://www.apprenticeships.org.uk/NR/rdonlyres/A28D2CFF–725E–4D00–9110–429A77CCA2C6/0/ApprenticeshipBlueprint FinalV215Sep05.pdf.

19 For an introduction to sector skills partnerships, see http://www.ssda.org.uk/ssda/default.aspx?page=1. Information on developments in the voluntary sector can be found at http://www.ssda.org.uk/ssda/PDF/041213%20PM%20MOU%20Final%20Draft%20VS%20with%20sigs.pdf

8

Fresh Churches and Emerging Expressions: Current Currents in the Oceans of Liquid Churches

Rev Joanne Cox

By this point in the book you may well be having one of several reactions. You may have stopped reading – in which case, you will not be reading this. You may be persuaded a little about the changing nature of church life and ministry, but still remain sceptical about its implications for leadership and deployment – in which case, this chapter is unlikely to sway you, but may challenge you a little more. You may be wholeheartedly convinced that 'the times they are a-changin' but retain little or no hope for the future of denominational leadership as it exists today – in which case, this chapter offers no swift solutions, but may offer some insight into where the Church in Britain (especially the Church of England and Methodism) are developing their theology, missiology and practice.

As a probationary Methodist minister who is under 30, I appear to fall in the tension outlined and exposed throughout this book. That is, the tension between being called into full-time Christian leadership within a denomination, and yet also feeling called to a ministry that extends beyond paperwork, pastoral care and what may crudely be described as palliative care for a dying church congregation. This chapter, therefore, is unique amongst the company of this book because it is written from the perspective of one who is 'emerging' within the stream of Methodism.

Kimball articulates the struggle that I and my contemporaries face when we risk entering into ordained leadership within established or denominational churches.

'Friction and misunderstanding develops among church leaders because those who are engaging a postmodern, post-Christian culture want to think about and design ministry differently. Many times the older pastors or leaders, being modern in their viewpoint, don't understand why a different methodology is needed.'[1]

This is not to say that the older pastors are wholly responsible, nor that either side in his statement is in any way better than the other. What this does indicate is that even before there is conflict in the pews, there is conflict in the team and in the wider church. Yet this conflict comes about because there is a clash of cultures, of identity, of worldviews and expectations. This is the tension in which the Bride of Christ resides at present.

This chapter seeks to dig a little deeper into what it means to be a 'church leader engaging in a postmodern, post-Christian culture' and what it means to 'think about and design ministry differently'. In order to do this, it is important initially to outline some of the terms that are used, adopted, adapted, and splashed around in any dialogue such as this. A brief description is thus provided for 'Emerging Church' and 'Fresh Expressions'. From this basis, a number of areas are outlined which represent significant features of leadership characteristics and training needs for those who fall into the liquid bracket of an emerging leader. Rather than being a prescription for the future these offer broad brushstrokes and some implicit questions. Key features will be 'is it safe?', specialist ministries and resources, re-digging spiritual wells, risk taking, apologetics, leadership, hero mentoring, and working at the fringes. This is not a complete list, but it does give a flavour of where the boundaries that have been clear-cut in the past are now being redefined, broken down and otherwise challenged both from those inside and, more vociferously, from those who no longer want to fight to do what they feel called and anointed to.

Defining the terms

It is somewhat ironic to spend time defining the terms; since the nature of what they describe is by definition undefinable. However, in an attempt to paint a broad landscape of the contemporary situation, there are two groupings that deserve a brief mention at this point. Emerging Church and Fresh Expression are the two most common terms, and yet often they are used synonymously. Although in specific cases this may be appropriate, this is not a universal understanding. Crucially, neither Fresh Expressions nor Emerging Church (or its cognate strategic wing Emergent) are denominations. In many ways neither actually exists.

Emerging Church

Emerging Church is a complex term: mainly because it does not exist as a single unified entity. The term 'Emerging Church' was coined by Karen Ward as her website domain. It was a means of her attempting to 'work through her questions about church'.[2] It has subsequently been adopted by a wide variety of people and contexts to describe this continuing conversation and investigation of what the kingdom of God might look like in the twenty-first century. It is far deeper and more complex than merely concluding that the Emerging Church is an attempt to make church experience culturally relevant, although the practical outcome of the Emerging Church often engages with specific cultures. This is seen, for example, in the engagement of club culture of the Nine O'Clock Service (NOS) in Sheffield during the early 1990s,[3] or the extension of this with 24/7 in Ibiza.[4] For now, the term *Emerging Church* refers to the smorgasbord of groups who are seeking to find an authentic way of living the Christian faith which takes seriously the present cultural climate, the impact of postmodern practice and philosophy, and which also recognizes the struggle and disillusionment with evangelicalism amongst a primarily Generation X and Y audience.

It is not to be confused with the think tank Emergent, which is quickly becoming a brand within the USA – a subdivision of Zondervan publishing, and an online network in the shape of Emergent Village. The Emerging Church is represented at Emergent, especially in people such as Tony Jones and Brian McLaren. Emergent is merely one part of the Emerging Church – a part which others wish to side step. As the Emergent website continues to develop its theological stream, it may well become more strategic in its influence in the USA.

Emerging Church spokespeople (for some do not want to be called 'leaders' or else deny that leadership structures should exist within community) share a diverse range of views and theologies; often negotiating and debating issues of orthodoxy and orthopraxis in person or in blog forums. The lack of named leaders means that there are a number of people who are adopted almost as gurus to the movement, and whose rhetoric and personality dominate conversation. In turn, it also means that some people are adopted as icons and influencers, but who would not seek to be part of the movement *per se*. This is seen especially through theological scholars such as of NT Wright and Walter Bruggemann, who are quoted time and again. Although sympathetic, neither Wright nor Bruggemann are Emerging Church practitioners. Indeed, Bishop Wright is fascinating, because as a member of the Establishment, he personifies many of the values that postmoderns have difficulty with: power, patriarchy, politics, wealth, etc.

Given that the Emerging Church seeks to move away from the dogmatic proclamations into a world of questions and investigation, it is no surprise that there is no contractual agreement to underline foundational theological agreements. The Emerging Church is not something that a church or organization can sign up to. It does not have a label or brand. Although creedal in belief, many would argue that dogma is open to debate and interpretation. Webber's compilation of five conversation partners in *Listening to the Beliefs of the Emerging Church* offers a useful insight into this world of theological gymnastics.[5] A serious challenge that this raises, however, is how to teach theology in such a way as to uphold orthodoxy, while at the same time not being afraid of creating heresy in the process of re-imagining orthodoxy.

There is no single source to explain what Emerging Churches look like, and no covenant to declare orthodoxy. However, Kimball has helpfully outlined nine features of Emerging Churches. Subsequent to publication this has continued to evolve, but it is a good starting place to recognize some of the key features pertaining to those community groups and congregations who would seek to adopt the label of Emerging Church.

Emerging Churches are communities that practice the way of Jesus within postmodern cultures. This definition encompasses the nine practices:

1. Identify with the life of Jesus
2. Transform the secular realm
3. Live highly communal lives

Because of these three activities, they:

4. Welcome the stranger
5. Serve with generosity
6. Participate as producers
7. Create as created beings
8. Lead as a body
9. Take part in spiritual activities.[6]

From this list, there is nothing that appears to be controversial or radical. Arguably, these are the features of the Church since its fiery birth at Pentecost. Indeed, the very notion of 'Emerging Church' has been around for the best part of 2,000 years.

A final word of caution is worth expressing in terms of Emerging Church discussions, namely that there is a difference between the USA and UK in this debate. The nature of Emerging Church is to be highly contextualized; to be incarnational in a specific place for a specific people means that what these nine points look like in reality will be very different. In turn, what this looks like in the UK, in which Christendom has been in decline for much of the last century, will be significantly different to the US context of megachurches and high church attendance.

Fresh Expressions

Having made a passing reference to the UK context, into the mix comes Fresh Expressions.

Following on from the *Mission-Shaped Church* report to the General Synod of the Church of England, the Archbishop of Canterbury, Rowan Williams, began an initiative called 'Fresh Expressions'.[7] In 2004, Steve Croft was appointed as Archbishop's Missioner to lead a team of Methodist and Anglican colleagues. Fresh Expressions was thus born, and has continued to evolve and develop in several strategic ways. Fresh Expressions runs a website database. Once registered, anyone can display details of a community or congregation who are seeking to develop a missionally focused way of being a Christian presence within their context. Fresh Expressions has also developed a series of training packages: from one-day events to a year-long programme. Initially, Fresh Expressions refused to define itself in a clear way, instead spending over a year trying to get an overview of where the Holy Spirit was at work in the UK. However, it is now well publicized that a Fresh Expression is

> Intended as a community or congregation which is, or has the potential to become, a church in its own right. It is not intended as a halfway house or stepping stone for someone joining a Sunday morning congregation.[8]

At the time of writing Fresh Expressions is entering its fifth year of existence and is thus seeking to develop new forms of ministry. Within the Anglican Church, this has already begun to happen with the development of Pioneer Ministers and the Order of Mission. Conversations are continuing as to how this is to impact Methodism.

Fresh Expressions as an organization, therefore, is a permission-giving body. It enables those who have innovative or creative ideas to take the risk at starting something new. There are hundreds of examples as to where this is currently being practised. There are some significant differences between Emerging Church and Fresh Expressions, and these need to be borne in mind in any discussion of contemporary church life. In terms of ecumenism, Fresh Expression is an Anglican-Methodist organization. As such, it comes under its discipline. Fresh Expressions is about the ecclesiology of mission (or the mission of ecclesiology). Whereas the starting point for Emerging Church is Christology and the Kingdom of God, Fresh Expressions remains missiologically fuelled. The ultimate journey may be the same, but the routes that are taken may be very different. Fresh Expressions is a brand. It is something that can be signed up to. It is a tangible 'thing' with a logo and a training package and a group of leaders. It is a structured and strategic entity in which the wider Church is invited to participate. Fresh Expressions is about change and evolution. It is about enabling and resourcing those who feel that the Spirit is moving a community in a specific direction for a specific group of people. It facilitates change from the inside. This contrasts significantly with some Emerging Church practices which are far more about leaving the past behind, and giving up on denominations altogether.

Implications

> It will provide God's people with a new sense of purpose, a divine connection to daily actions. We need to grasp the fact that in God's economy our actions do have an eternal impact. We do extend the kingdom of God in daily affairs and activities and actions done in the name of Jesus.[9]

As has been indicated, in the midst of the current leadership quagmire, there are a number of terms that are used to describe the current ecclesial *Zeitgeist*. Each one is a slippery entity: constantly changing and creating within an individual context. It is easy to be hypnotized by the terminology so much that the practical implications and experiences become an after-thought. With this in mind, it is important that the permanence of text, however liquid or organic, does not replace listening to, watching and learning from the people this book describes. Despite what your experience of church might be on a Sunday morning, these people are not hard to find. It is often the case that they are not in your church building at all. Controversially, they may never be – and that is OK. These are the people who are the pioneers, the entrepreneurs, the visionaries. They are those who voluntarily, tirelessly and sacrificially work and work and work (and who are humble enough for no one to ever notice). You will see them in coffee shops, shopping centres, hostels, protests, pubs, clubs, shoe shops, and Tesco. Watch out for these people, for theirs is the Kingdom of God – and they want everyone else to know about it! There is nothing that can replace conversation, engagement and open, honest dialogue. Such intentional engagement may well be the catalyst from which the glowing embers of Christian community and the Kingdom of God will be reignited.

Ultimately, whatever terms you use for the wider change in church life and leadership; whatever the implications are for the way that Jesus is worshipped and glorified by His people; whatever the Spirit is doing in the places where you are reading this book, this cannot be merely cosmetic surgery. Questions about leadership training, deployment, and employment are one side of a larger multi-dimensional issue: that of the nature of God, and what that means for us His people. Removing pews, fixing a protector and screen, removing or rewriting hymnbooks or deliberately employing 'postmoderns' or 'young people' will not herald in the kingdom of God in the long term. They are good ideas and can be put to good use for the sake of the Kingdom; but they are not the solution.

Training for Fresh Emerging Church Expressions

As has been indicated thus far, the ecclesio-cultural milieu is a complex one. In the midst of this Godly chaos, there are a huge number of implications for the training of those leaders who feel called to work within it. This is not to say that the current training packages are unsuitable for the task. However, there is a growing sense that the training currently offered does not provide all the tools necessary to work in this new world. In no way is this an exhaustive list, but neither is it an attempt to deny the benefit gained from training. However, with Emerging Church and Fresh Expressions comes a new list of training needs; alongside a group of leaders who are spiritually and practically equipped in different ways. No longer is the one-size-fits-all 'vicar factory' approach sufficient for these pioneers and visionaries. Indeed, very few have the energy or the inclination to jump through the necessary hoops in order to be in a place of influence where they can remove the hoops for others.

Is it safe?

'Safe?' said Mr Beaver; 'Don't you hear what Mrs Beaver tells you? Who said anything about safe? 'Course he isn't safe. But he is good. He's the King I tell you.'[10]

'He's like fire and ice, and rage. He's like the night, and the storm in the heart of the sun. He's ancient and forever. He burns at the centre of time and he can see the turn of the universe. And he's wonderful.'[11]

As has already been noted, the challenges of ecclesiology and leadership are indicative of a deeper challenge to the nature and understanding of God. One could be easily forgiven for thinking that the god of modernism was into the interior design of the Gothic to Victorian periods, enjoyed opera and was quite fond of close harmonies. The point of the aesthetics of buildings is to give an impression of the God to whom worship is offered. A challenge thus offered by fresh ways of expressing worship, is that it is the community, the group of people, who reflect this. They are the image of God, not a high altar or statue or plaque. Releasing God from the bricks and mortar is a reminder that the God we worship – the Creator, Son and Holy Spirit – is dangerous.

In lieu of the headlines about those who misuse their leadership positions, safety in terms of protocols and policies are increasingly important. Indeed, one development in terms of training may well have to include more business-orientated writing of policy documents. What this good practice should not do, however, is confuse the safety of the community with a lack of risk and change.

Too often our concepts of God are neutered. Childhood images of God are like our dad – Jesus is blond, blue-eyed and slender, the Holy Spirit only mentioned in passing. Theology is resigned to being (dare it be written?) too safe. Once church is made safe, then God becomes safe too. The church is good at being safe. Worship is ordered and structured and repeated. Events are planned to consider all perspectives and not to offend anyone. Ecclesiological governance is authenticated through charter and constitution and legally binding documents. Buildings are insured, people are checked, members are listed and children are registered. And as the daily business (and busy-ness) goes on, it becomes more easy to be safe than to be good.

In relying upon maintaining the *status quo*, making sure that the language of policies are just right, in keeping up to date with legal twists and turns, it is easy to lose the very mission of the Kingdom of God that they're meant to enable. God has been made so safe that He is bound in red tape and filed in a corner, rather than letting the Lion of Judah prowl.

The challenge raised is thus to create somewhere that is safe for those who have no history or experience of 'church'; but which may be risky and frightening for those who have been involved in the modernistic forms of church and community. There has been a complete turn around (could one say 'repentance' at this point?) from church as liked by those who have been involved for years and decades, to the missional centre required if Christian community is to effectively engage with contemporary cultures and peoples. Instead of being a place of shelter from the outside world, the challenge for congregations and training institutions is to encourage the discernment of ways in which space can be created to allow others to meet with God. With this may well come legal precautions and policies that are there for the benefit of all who are a part of the community. The overarching challenge is to equip leaders with the ability to strategically – meant in terms of creating space – enable people to meet with God on their own terms.

In turn, there is a further challenge which says that Christian leadership is not a 'safe' thing. Although there is no such thing as the 'emerging generation' (because every generation emerges at some point in history), there are features of the leadership styles within Emerging Church and Fresh Expressions which also rely on God being good, but not on church being safe. This is a generation of entrepreneurs, visionaries, activists, revolutionaries, pioneers, and missionaries who are breaking new ground and resurrecting vintage Christian practices. These are not a group of people who are looking for job security. They are not looking for a job for life – although vocationally, Christian service is life-long. Many are seeking second jobs in order to subsidize their community work. In this way, part time training courses are being developed to enable this to continue. Further work on issues of job-sharing, volunteer leadership and 'tent-making', needs to be undertaken. This is especially the case as leaders become employed as lay people and as finances become stretched within the institutions.

Inspired by accounts of the persecuted church in the forgotten corners of the globe, these leaders are also increasingly aware of the impending reality of persecution for themselves too. The challenge is to create an environment in which the worldwide church is a part of life. A place where the stories of martyrs are told, and those in similar situations are interceded for. Christianity did not begin as something safe. It was an underground movement. Reclaiming some of this past and appropriating it for the present is a key component of ministry and will continue to be so as long as the church community remains open to the plight of the marginalized and the outcast, the asylum seeker and the refugee.

As Greig prophetically graffitied on a prayer-room wall:

> They are free from materialism – they laugh at 9–5 little prisons. They could eat caviar on Monday and crusts on Tuesday – they wouldn't even notice.[12]

This is not a vocation to a job-secure, life-long, house-provided, hymn-sandwich, middle class, suburban dream. The call of these leaders is to something other than that, and the training will need to shift to match the godly intentions offered by these good and dangerously safe people. One guarantee is that it will be chaotic. It will be messy. It might not feel safe. But it will be good.

Specialists

> The reality is that mainstream culture no longer brings people to the church door. We can no longer assume that we can automatically reproduce ourselves, because the pool of people who regard the church as relevant or important is decreasing with every generation.[13]

Williams coined the phrase 'mixed economy' in the course of the *Mission-Shaped Church* discussions, meaning that Christian community needed to be incarnated and planted in different ways for different people within the same geography. This has been nuanced slightly in recent months with the adoption of the phrase 'mixed ecology' which gives a sense of evolution and growth in its appropriation. Be it an economy from commerce or an ecology from nature, what is stressed is the move towards a more specialized form of community. No longer is there a one-size-fits-all option. Rather the challenge for leaders and community alike is to discover what it means for them to be the unique and appropriate incarnation of the Kingdom of God in a specific place (and for a specific time). Frost and Hirsch note this when they reflect that 'mission is always conditioned by that act whereby God reached out to us in a meaningful way when he moved into our neighbourhood'.[14] It is this reaching out into the neighbourhood that is continued in this mixed ecology of the Kingdom.

The exciting challenge of this is that, 'there will be as many forms [of missional church] as there are subcultures or people groups or neighbourhoods to reach'.[15] Communities will evolve through networks. The implication of this is that as training becomes specific to individuals, it also shifts to being specific to vocation, location and/or gifting. With this comes the need to read and know a community intimately, to be involved in the flows of people and the transitions that are a part of daily life. It demands that the resources are made available so that national and global networks can be formed for like-minded people in similar situations. Psychologically it means that leaders need to be extroverts – or at least told how to be extrovert – to be able to engage with people outside a shop, at a skate park, in a car park or during the bridge championship at the local women's meeting.

One Sunday morning John Smith walks into his local church. He is greeted at the door by a friendly but brusque lady who shakes his hand, welcomes him into the church. She does this without averting her eyes from the pile of books and leaflets that are on her right, as she tries to prise the set away for John. With arms now full of a notice sheet (containing information which will be repeated again at the start of the service), a hymnbook, a service book, and an additional song sheet, John carefully shuffles his way into the main building. Creeping down the central aisle, his feet – surrounded as they are by the latest Converse – still make a noise on the wooden floorboards. In an effort not to stand out any more, John decides to sit at the back of the church. Having negotiated the handbags that have already been placed on the pew, John figures that there is a space at the end of the row under the stained-glass window. He sits down. Slowly he discovers that the pew is not only under the stained glass window, but that the icon is leaky. Now with stained GAP jeans, John moves forwards to the next available pew. The service begins. Hymns displayed on the wooden hymn board are sung with the usual British gusto, at a tempo either slightly too slow or slightly too fast for the congregation to manage, although you could not tell as the organ volume drowns out any irregularities. That is, other than the couple sat behind him, whose joint operatic vibrato and off-key harmonies explain why this pew was available. Monosyllabic prayers are not easily differentiated from the vanilla sermon. One hour, five hymns, one psalm, two readings, and a children's address later, John exits the building. Or at least attempts to, until, after shaking hands with the preacher, he is ushered into a side room to enjoy tepid tea and digestive biscuits. With stained jeans, noisy shoes and a bruised hand, John leaves quietly and unnoticed.

This may well have been your experience on Sunday morning. If not, then it is a caricature to which you are likely to relate to. What it attempts to illustrate is the replicability of what 'church' means to those whose experience is no different to our poor John Smith. That such a caricature can be drawn means that the reality is somewhat close to it.

In a mixed ecology, however, John may attend the Monday morning prayer breakfast before he gets on a train to London where he will spend most of the week. The youth group will meet after the football match for a drink in the local pub, where Mark will tell everyone about his sister who is in hospital at the moment, and the team will offer to visit her. Margaret will arrange the flowers for the women's group meeting who in turn will be planning their annual pilgrimage to Iona. Ethan will play happily in the playgroup on a Tuesday morning, whilst his mum Hannah discusses the theological themes in this week's edition of 'Lost' in the hall next door. Abby runs an Alpha course for the young offenders that she volunteers with. Andrew offers music therapy for the local old people's home. Amy is going snowboarding on mission.

No longer does the stereotype ring true – or at least, it does on a Sunday morning, but that is only a fraction of the ecclesiological, missiological and Christological picture. Christian community exists in diversity. That this diversity is now tangible on every street corner is challenging the Church to make this reality tangible in its building of communities and networks. Being comfortable with difference and not anticipating that a service will have something for everyone is a significant cultural shift.

As the structures change, especially in terms of Methodist circuits and districts, it will be interesting to see how these networks of communities are recognized, resourced and released by the wider church. Specialists have been a part of recognized ordained ministry in a number of areas: sector work, chaplaincy, evangelism, and training, to name but a few. Questions remain as to how this evolves when the networks include Chinese-speaking churches, alternative worship communities, new monasticism, sector-based children's work, drug counselling, homelessness, knitting groups, and the local scat poets society. These questions are not only in terms of releasing leaders to serve these specific and individual communities, but also how evangelism and worship is understood within them and then reflected back into the Catholic Church to which they belong. Different ecclesiological and leadership issues will be raised by each community, bringing with it treasures to share and gravel to sift through if any progress is to be made in the mixed ecology. If the Church has one great need it is this: to be set free for the Kingdom of God, to be liberated from what it has become in order to be itself as God intends.

Spiritual wells

> Jesus loves his bride in any structure or model in which she is found. I often counsel young idealists in our movement, 'don't bash the bride no matter how ugly she looks to you. If you start attacking the bride, sooner or later you're going to have to take on the Groom, and I don't think you want that!'[16]

One of the most favoured Bible passages that are used and commented upon in regards to missional church development is that of the parable of the wineskins (Mt. 9:17; Mk. 2:22; Lk. 5:37). But the implication of this in terms of fresh ways of being church is that the old wineskin is defunct and cannot contain the new product. This may seem like the obvious solution, leave the old wine in its old wineskins until it is drunk or else it goes off, and work on creating new wine skins for the new wine. It is easy sometimes to forget that there is value in the vintage wine too. One risk with creative and innovative new ideas is that the past practices are dismissed without a second thought. It is with this in mind that

Kimball reflects, 'in the Emerging Church we need to bring back the ancient symbols and talk about the Jewish roots of our faith'.[17] Not only do leaders need to get an insight into the context of the biblical texts; what is required is a deeper understanding of the traditional practices that go with them, the rituals and the parties, the laments and the storytelling.

Whereas Frost and Hirsch begin their thesis with the firm belief that a new reformation or revolution is required for new generations, the rediscovery of monasticism, celtic spirituality (and indeed any form of spirituality), holiness movements, covenant-based accountability circles and the like indicate that there are deep spiritual wells that need to be dug out, their living waters allowed to break free once again (Gen. 26).

Something new may well rise out of the ashes of the past, but it is also possible that something beloved will be resurrected for the present day. The spiritual inheritance of the UK is not always something to be proud of, and to a greater extent it is the seeds of the past that are being reaped today, a harvest of decline and disillusionment. In discerning the rhythms and patterns to which the Spirit is calling His people, it may also be necessary to confess the transgressions of the past. Leaders must thus tell the story of people and places as it is; with honesty and integrity, and divine those spiritual wells to refresh and inspire growth in the present day. As Frost and Hirsch state,

> creativity as such adds value to knowledge by providing a meaningful interface, a medium of accessibility, for the user of knowledge. In this function, creativity adds new meanings to old activities and rituals; it reinterprets and restores old and outworn symbols and gives them currency and meaning.[18]

The task of creatively engaging with rituals and symbols involves careful story keeping, listening and re-imagining what could be from what is. This is often not a skill that can be taught or learnt. The power of memory and the skills to listen and to reinterpret are all cognate tools in a leaders' kit. The juxtaposition remains that

> Today's mass media are the windows of our culture. They provide the myths – the stories and images – that explain to us who we are ...

in other words, the worldview that explains, unites and guides our lives[19]

rather than the scriptures and hymnody of yore.

Be it a case of making new wineskins or digging wells, the bride of Christ may not be perfect in this time and place. Yet the resources and the lessons and the stories are there. The past is not something to be dislocated from the present reality or future eschatological hope. Discernment and prayerful investment remains at the top of a leader's to-do list.

Taking risks

> We were here before you and we will stay longer than you are going to.

Such was the greeting made to one student who dared to bring a projector, computer and screen into the church for worship one Sunday morning. Training institutions are good at allowing space for students to practice. There is space for things to go brilliantly well, and safety and security if they go horribly wrong. Yet in the scary wide world outside of peer support such a culture often ceases to exist.

As innovative and creative ways of developing Christian community continue to evolve, it is becoming increasingly necessary for leaders to be trained in how to create a culture of change making and risk taking. This is hugely demanding for those in leadership, because it means being prepared to step out and try something even when people are not keen on an idea. It means being open to comments and criticism as well as celebration. It means having in place a form of review. And it means having the integrity of heart to be honest about something if it is not working. Taking risks offers the expectation that something will succeed, and the preparation that sometimes things just do not work.

With this comes the added responsibility of being able to effectively communicate to as many people as possible. It may require the marketing skills of a leader as well as pastoral wisdom. Entrepreneurs also struggle with the long-term view. In this way, those who are prepared to take risks also require the skills to mentor and develop leaders from within, so as to enable the continuing development of community after their energy has dissipated.

When it comes to taking risks, perhaps one of the key features of ministry will be the development of support networks. If modern church is good at doing anything, it is unfortunately excellent at disenchanting leaders. Building up support networks and facilitating good avenues and practices for feedback are essential for the psychological wellbeing of those in leadership. Although not exclusive, it is possible that this is more of a feature for women in leadership. Networks of encouragement and support will be vital for the long-term vision and energy of a leader.

A sub-section to a culture of risks is the increasing significance of civil and sector partnerships. As partners such as SureStart and Local Authorities use premises and develop community-based projects, leaders become more than spiritual guides for a community. They become the fundraiser, the chair of the management committee, and the centre manager. There are thus gaps in training about how to deal with the civil and sector worlds, and how to manage effectively when one is called to minister in the gap between these and the spiritual realms.

Apologetics

> It is this tension [between the church and the world] that God calls us to – an intersection of culture and communication. Incarnational ministry of this magnitude can be done, done well, and in a way that both honours and glorifies God. Jesus pulled it off.[20]

It has already been mentioned that communication is intrinsic to leadership and vocation in the twenty-first century. This needs to be developed further to encapsulate the need to have a concrete hermeneutic for the interpretation of culture. The ever-increasing use of mass media as well as the development of online communities and networks requires that leaders and community members have the necessary tools to affirm, critique, subvert, and interpret for the worship of God and the benefit of the Christian community. The apologetic task remains crucial in the resourcing of evangelists and leaders. As mass media communication evolves into the social networking world, and as personal entertainment systems become social substitutes, an inoculation against technophobia will be part of the course.

McGrath states, 'the chief goal of Christian apologetics is to create an intellectual and imaginative climate conducive to the birth and nurture of faith'.[21] The use of mass media, therefore, is deeper than making an event 'seeker friendly'. It is about enabling spiritual questions to be asked, and having the trust and the platform in which to nurture discipleship from that common grounding. It is not a reduction of the gospel; it is an elevation of the task of the prophet and the evangelist to be able to wisely consume culture but not to be consumed by it. The world of emerging cultures and fresh expressions is one in which 'out there' is more attractive than the 'in here' of the Church. Engaging with the wider world demands specific training in the use, abuse, and misuse of cultural icons and ideas – and the means through which these can all be gainfully employed in the personal quest for the Kingdom.

Christ-centred conversation is more likely to happen discussing a Greenday, Linkin Park or Kanye West lyric, than over a digestive biscuit. Pastoral care is not the once-a-year visit from the pastor, but the weekly coffee, pint after work, or movie post-mortem. This is not a new concept. Wesley's social holiness encouraged social engagement, poverty eradication, and small group Bible studies (we may now call them cells) to deepen discipleship and to bring people to faith. Evangelism happens when friends realize that the Jesus of all those childhood stories is relevant for them. In reality Cinderella may not get to the ball (or if she does, she will not get the prince), sleeping beauty remains comatose and George's dragon is on the rampage. But Jesus, He becomes more than the myth. He becomes the example, the author and perfector of faith – the prince, the knight and the dragon slayer (whatever dragons need slaying: be they self harm, an eating disorder, domestic violence, debt, alcohol or drug abuse, overwork, depression – the list goes on). Jesus is removed from those Victorian pictures with the blue eyes and the long blonde hair, and instead is seen biblically as the storyteller, rule breaker, miracle worker, healer, teacher, soul carer, and intercessor. It is this core of Christ, to whom many are now deeply attracted. As Moby wrote in his blog at Christmas 2006, christ compels us to be better than we usually are.

christ compels us to forgive those who've wronged us.

christ compels us to love our enemies.

christ compels us to be humble and non-judgemental.

christ compels us to care for the neediest.

christ compels us to be non-violent.

christ compels us to recognize that the material world and all of our posessions will ultimately turn into dust, so we shouldn't get too attached to our bodies, our lives, and our stuff.

and, most importantly (in many ways), christ compels us to love one another and look after one another, and to see all people as our own family.

so when i call myself a christian it's because i find christ's character and teachings to be incredibly compelling and, well, divine (cos they're too weird/impractical/perfect to have ever been invented by a human being).

all of the other stuff: virgin birth, apocryphal gospels, did christ have a wife/brother/twin/dog/etc?,

i find to be interesting window dressing.

if someone came to me and said: 'i have proof that there was no virgin birth and that christ had a brother and a wife and a boston terrier!' i'd say: 'ok. but his teachings are still pretty remarkable, regardless of the circumstances of his life, right?'[22]

Jesus, not the Church, is the source of postmodern identity. The church is not the attractive element. In a world that vies for celebrity and personal identity crises the inherent message is that individuals want to be noticed: there is an open door to bringing the Jesus of the text alive to people. His life and teaching makes sense. The challenge, especially for the evangelical wing of the Church, is to relocate the story of His death and resurrection in the perception that Jesus was a good man from whom things can be learnt and applied today. In contemporary cultures, therefore, leadership within a community that does not define itself by building or by networks brings significant challenges both to existing communities and to the institutions that train them. It also asks serious questions about leadership, vision and organization.

A nuance to the apologetic task is that crossing cultural barriers need not be about technology, Apple Macs, DVDs, and literature surveys. This is, as has been indicated above, a crucial part of engaging and understanding people today. Yet, the implication of discussing the juxtaposition of modernism and postmodernism is that there is also a cross-cultural gap in education along the lines of missionaries traversing the globe. There are great lessons to learn from Storti's work in crossing cultures and self-understanding.[23] Cultural differences within a locality can cause as much culture shock as crossing an ocean. Again, this is an area where there has been little to no research. Silence does not mean that it is not significant, however. Questions of how to read and understand the cultural use of emotion, language, gestures, time keeping, and etiquette are increasingly important for leaders to recognize and to be able to adapt to within a given scenario.

Leadership

> If we could do church all over again, we would build clear leadership philosophy and vision, recognising that imaginative, godly, biblical leadership is absolutely vital. It is *the* strategic area of leverage for change.[24]

Leadership is thus one of the most fundamental issues facing the continuing development of Christian community in the twenty-first century. In order for change to come about in the way that church is practice, community is built and the gospel shared, the first thing that needs to evolve is the leadership. This is the contention of Frost and Hirsch's seminal work *The Shaping of Things to Come,* which sits as one of the foremost contributors to the current debate about the nature and role of leadership within the world of Emerging Church. Such conclusions have led them to conclude that leadership in a new guise for forthcoming generations cannot come from within a denomination. They note, 'the kind of thinking that will solve the world's problems will be of a different order to the kind of thinking that created them in the first place'.[25] The challenge remains for those within established and denominational churches to wrestle with this conclusion and to respond in ways which perhaps stand against the conclusion to bail out.

A significant problem when it comes to the contemporary practice of priestly ministry, especially that of Presbyteral ministry in the Methodist Church, is that those who are ordained often do not see themselves as leaders at all. The role of pastor and servant is so ingrained in the models that are available that those who are in positions of influence are not those who have the legally binding authority within a community. Those who are ordained are manipulated by those within the congregation, or they are not supported when they want to do something new. They do not have the skills with which to communicate or to innovate new ideas. Yet they are well loved by the congregations because they do what is expected of them, they visit the membership list regularly and they attend the coffee morning.

In terms of training, there is a need to focus upon leadership in more detail – and to facilitate more entrepreneurial, visionary and risky patterns of leadership. One feature may also be to develop mentoring packages, resourcing future leaders from the experience and gifting that is already tried and tested within the emerging and Fresh Expressions scene. This needs to go beyond titles and hoop-jumping. Lessons for leadership need to be intensely and uniquely Christian while at the same tile uniquely suited to the particular requirements of the context. Leaders may need to be re-trained in an on-going development scheme. They also need to be resourced to be able to invest within the community; raising up leaders from within rather than relying on stationing committees and advertising in order to appoint someone to serve in a ministerial capacity.

Adopt a hero

> You can benefit by learning from the lives, ideas and actions of the great geniuses of history. Adopt a role model.[26]

Three of my heroes are: Russell T. Davis, a brilliantly creative mind who has been involved in bringing to television screens iconic characters and edgy series; Rob Lacey, who, despite losing a long battle with cancer, was able to bring scriptures to life through poetry and drama; and Queen Elizabeth I, a phenomenal woman who transformed the face of the world, and still retained mystery, femininity and ambition. A significant shift in contemporary vocation discernment is the use of cultural icons rather than biblical characters, in the process. It is increasingly common for testimonies to refer to chart music, TV shows and films, rather than to parables and books of the Bible. Alongside apologetic dexterity, therefore, there is also a growing desire to inject Christological examples into a vocational framework. In a world in which God communicates through mass media and through visual icons, there is the impending potential to unlock the scriptures afresh. This is especially true for a generation of school children whose religious education fails in this regard. Biblical leaders are not part of the vocational account because often the stories are not known.

With 'new' forms of leadership comes a wholesale change in thinking and the way ideas are brought to birth. This can include the ability to survive by asking questions and living with a multitude of answers, the willingness to do something to see if it works, the creativity to search for inspiration in unexpected places and the desire to seek out people who challenge the *status quo*. The theory of adopting a hero is two-fold. Firstly, it may enable a leader to respond in an uncharacteristic way in a situation. This is partly because they may see a different solution, and partly because it is possible to think in another person's shoes. Secondly, and more significantly, it unlocks the secret of mentoring. One of the key features for emerging leaders is the ability to watch and learn from the admired and the 'successful' – not only in terms of those in fiction, history or public life. It is also a factor in the training of leaders who are able to watch and learn from those who have been there and done that. It also enables a theological reflection upon problem solving and mistake making. Leaders are not perfect. No leader ever was. It is easy to adopt a hero mentality, rather than be discipled by practitioners and discipled and disciplined by Jesus.

Fringe living

Perhaps one of the key, and yet unarticulated, differences between Emerging Church and Fresh Expressions is that Emerging

Church pioneers are used to existing on the fringes of church communities. They have all the war wounds to show for their battles. The popularity of Fresh Expressions has the potential to erase some of the memory of hard won battles with authorities and congregations. However, the boundaries are changing. Emerging Church theory itself has been emerging for the best part of 20 years. Fresh Expressions is now common parlance and an extremely popular brand onto which all sorts of things are attached. The mission-shaped bandwagon is racing its way through the tumbleweed-inhabited churches in the UK. But what happens if the bell-curve is already on its downturn. Where next for the entrepreneur? If this is where the Church is now discussing its middle ground, the question has to be asked: where is this going? Where is the long-term vision, and how is continuing training and development enabling this question to be both asked and answered?

As the mainstream now anticipates and expects courageous and outlandish things of its 'young' or even pioneer-ordained leaders (be they priests or deacons), the fringe and the cutting edge has moved. But where to? While it is now trendy and well resourced to place one's vocation and ministry, where are the next pioneers. The difficulty is that training and leadership theory will not have caught up to the present-day needs, before new questions are asked in a completely different arena. The nature of society today is such that things change quickly. Without prophets and visionaries to remain constantly at the fringes, it is hard to foresee a pathway into the future.

The problem with being on the fringes is that one gets used to persecution and estrangement, whether a thousand backbiting comments, a dozen arguments about decisions, or individuals who disagree in council meetings and PCCs which in turn mean that the new is not supported in the vote. Working on the fringe is a lot easier to do if there is no middle ground to appease, to be accountable to, and to serve. The middle ground is a safe place to live so long as most of the people are pleased for most of the time. The personality and character of a leader who is willing to bridge the gap between the middle ground and the fringes has to be a person who can deal well with criticism, who can defend both parties and who can negotiate and navigate different routes and journey's. Just as they should not fall into the trap of superhero syndromes, the task is to resource leaders with the psychological tools to maintain wellbeing of mind and spirit that can last the course when it seems that everyone disagrees. This may require professional and specialized counsellors. It may need the strength and security of accountability partnerships. It will certainly mean the development and implementation of collaborative ministry. And it requires a shared vision for the future which is dependent upon God, and not the individual characters.

Fringes can be the forgotten places. Fresh Expressions and Emerging Church practice are bringing the fringes into the spotlight. But this means that there will be new fringes. The task is to seek those out too, and to be bold enough to stand firm in vision and values despite the voice of the other.

The last word

I leave the final words to Kimball

> I beg all who desire to have an impact in the Emerging Church to be 'shrewd as snakes', thinking strategically, studying the culture, and functioning as missiologists like never before. We need to be the poets, theologians, and philosophers once again. We need not be afraid to rethink everything we are doing. We need to set the pace for social justice in our communities and be thinking globally. We need to be fluid when we lead, instead of being rigid or controlling. We need to be relational leaders instead of super-soul-driven-leaders. But please, please, please, above all, pay ruthless attention to the prayerful care of your souls as leaders. Live holy and pure lives as innocent as doves in a corrupt and polluted culture. Be constantly connected to the chief Shepherd of the Emerging Church for his leading and guidance. Nothing is more important than this. Nothing.[27]

Vocation, training and vision are nothing if not rooted steadfast and sure in an intimate and integral relationship the Creator God, through the saving Son, Jesus Christ, resourced through the Holy Spirit. This is the creedal theology, the cornerstone, the ultimate vision and the discipline which fuels true Christian community wherever it is to be found.

Bibliography

Cole, Neil, *Organic Church: Growing Faith Where Life Happens* (San Francisco, CA: Jossey-Bass, 2005).

Cray, Graham, et al., *Mission-Shaped Church* (London: Church House, 2004).

Fore, William F., *Mythmakers: Gospel, Culture and the Media* (New York, NY: Friendship, 1990).

Frost, Michael, and Alan Hirsch, *The Shaping of Things to Come* (Peabody, MA: Hendrickson, 2003).

Gibbs, Eddie and Ryan Bolger, *Emerging Churches* (London: SPCK, 2006).

Greig, Pete, *The Vision and the Vow* (London: Kingsway, 2004).

Kimball, Dan, *The Emerging Church: Vintage Christianity for New Generations* (Grand Rapids, MI: Zondervan, 2003).

Lewis, C.S., *The Lion, the Witch and the Wardrobe* (London: Lion, 1980).

Pillinger, Pete and Andrew Roberts, *Changing Church for a Changing World* (Peterborough: Epworth, 2007).

Storti, Craig, *The Art of Crossing Cultures* (Boston, MA: Nicholas Brealey, 2nd edn, 2000).

—, *Figuring Foreigners Out* (Boston, MA: Nicholas Brealey, 2nd edn, 2000).

Sweet, Leonard (ed.), *The Church in Emerging Culture* (Grand Rapids, MI: Emergent, Zondervan, 2003).

Webber, Robert, *Listening to the Beliefs of the Emerging Church* (Grand Rapids, MI: Zondervan, 2007).

Other Sources

God Bless Ibiza, Channel 4 Productions, 2003.

Doctor Who, *Family of Blood*, BBC Productions, 2007.

Moby's Christmas Message (http://www.moby.com/journal/2006–12–21/i_think_its_odd_funny_when_people_come_t.html).

Notes

[1] Kimball, Dan, *The Emerging Church: Vintage Christianity for New Generations* (Grand Rapids, MI: Zondervan, 2003), 65.

[2] Gibbs, Eddie and Ryan Bolger, *Emerging Churches* (London: SPCK, 2006), 30.

3 See Gibbs and Bolger, *Emerging Churches,* 82–7.
4 See 'God Bless Ibiza' Channel 4 Productions, 2003.
5 Webber, Robert, *Listening to the Beliefs of the Emerging Church* (Grand Rapids, MI: Zondervan, 2007).
6 Gibbs and Bolger, *Emerging Churches,* 45.
7 Cray, Graham, et al., *Mission-Shaped Church* (London: Church House, 2004).
8 Pillinger, Pete and Andrew Roberts, *Changing Church for a Changing World* (Peterborough: Epworth, 2007), 17.
9 Frost, Michael, and Alan Hirsch, *The Shaping of Things to Come* (Peabody, MA: Hendrickson, 2003), 115.
10 Lewis, C.S., *The Lion, the Witch and the Wardrobe* (London: Lion, 1980), 75.
11 Doctor Who, *Family of Blood*, BBC Productions, 2007.
12 Greig, Pete, *The Vision and the Vow* (London: Kingsway, 2004), 201.
13 Cray, Graham, et al., *Mission-Shaped Church,* 11.
14 Frost and Hirsch, *Shaping,* 58.
15 Frost and Hirsch, *Shaping,* 30.
16 Cole, Neil, *Organic Church: Growing Faith where Life Happens* (San Francisco, CA: Jossey-Bass, 2005), 139.
17 Kimball, Dan, *Emerging Churches,* 149.
18 Frost and Hirsch, *Shaping,* 186.
19 Fore, William F., *Mythmakers: Gospel, Culture and the Media* (New York, NY: Friendship, 1990), 51.
20 McManus, Erwin, 'The Global Intersection' in Sweet, Leonard (ed.), *The Church in Emerging Culture* (Grand Rapids, MI: Emergent, Zondervan, 2003), 258.
21 McGrath, A., *Bridge-Building* (Leicester: InterVarsity Press, 1994), 9.
22 Moby's Christmas Message http://www.moby.com/journal/2006–12–21/i_think_its_odd_funny_when_people_come_t.html viewed on 15 January 2007.
23 Storti, Craig, *The Art of Crossing Cultures* (Boston, MA: Nicholas Brealey, 2nd edn, 2000) and *Figuring Foreigners Out* (Boston, MA: Nicholas Brealey, 2nd edn, 2000).
24 Frost and Hirsch, *Shaping,* 67.
25 Frost and Hirsch, *Shaping,* 189.
26 Frost and Hirsch, *Shaping,* 198.
27 Kimball, *Emerging Church,* 248.

9

Pentecostal Perspectives on College Education

Dr Keith Warrington

Background

For most of their existence, Pentecostal Bible Colleges have been venues for short-term preparation for ministry, not places for exploration and contemplation. Studies were not expected to last longer than two years and were often much shorter, the teachers often being successful or experienced ministers or evangelists. Not all the teaching was of a high quality nor was it intended to provide an opportunity for discourse or analysis. McClung writes of study conducted there as, 'more experiential than cognitive, more activist than reflective, more actualized than analysed'.[1] The major purpose for the establishment of such colleges was to prepare people for evangelism and leading churches rather than for objective enquiry and development of Pentecostal scholarship.[2] Also, in the early days of Pentecostalism, there was a strong belief in the imminent return of Jesus and therefore to engage in extended periods of study was felt to be inappropriate.[3] Similarly, in the (positive) quest for evangelism, education has generally suffered; worship and the place of the emotions has been elevated but the place of the intellect in worship has concomitantly been sidelined; and while church growth has emphasized the status of the pastor/preacher, the teacher has been marginalized. Such a context causes Palmer to call for a return to the fundamental *raison d'etre* of the believer – to commune with the Creator, as a result of which the creation of a Christian worldview becomes paramount;[4] such a challenging and responsible objective is potentially best served in a Theological College setting. In an interesting empirical investigation, Kay demonstrates that, as recently as 1999, 36 per cent of UK Pentecostal ministers had not received any formal theological training while only 10 per cent had gained a degree in theology.[5]

In recent years, there has been considerable discussion by Pentecostals concerning the role and development of Bible Colleges and Christian education.[6] In some areas of the world, there has been a resurgence in the growth of Pentecostal Bible Colleges and scholarship.[7] However, in other regions, this has not been reflected, Sepúlveda, for example, describing Chilean Pentecostals as still exhibiting a 'strong anti-theological, anti-academic prejudice'.[8] Similarly, Hedlund cautions against this tendency among some Indian Pentecostals[9] as does Ayuk of Nigerian Pentecostals.[10] This propensity is often most espoused where the leaders are less educated as well as where the perception of ministerial success is viewed as being solely or significantly due to the Spirit.[11] In general, Pentecostals have preferred to live in contexts dominated by exclamation rather than questions marks.

However, there have been significant developments in Pentecostal education. The concept of teaching in the Pentecostal Church is being increasingly recognized as crucially important to its wellbeing. Although theological reflection in the early decades of Pentecostalism was often defensive, reactionary, intermittent and narrow in scope, the more recent decades have seen a marked increase in scholarship and exploration by Pentecostals of issues relating to their theology, spirituality and history. Bowdle encourages this development, noting that 'Jesus is Lord of learning'.[12]

Pentecostals are redeeming the concept of scholarship, enabling and encouraging those who have been so gifted to engage in it for the benefit of the Church, the development and training of leaders[13] and the exploration of doctrinal truths.[14] The importance of reflection and studious thinking has never been more necessary nor more available in Pentecostalism with a number of significant Pentecostal journals and societies having been established towards the close of the twentieth century.[15] There was a time when the term 'Pentecostal scholar' was viewed as an oxymoron. It is now much more acceptable to acknowledge that one's intellect is God-given and that it can be used for the glory of God in the context of teaching and research.[16] Allied with the Spirit, a powerful combination is anticipated.

Colleges are increasingly recognizing that they are not meant to be places where sacred Pentecostal dogmas are safeguarded at the expense of encouraging students to think about their beliefs. Learning needs to be more than simply receiving and reproducing information. It is the exploration of truth (not simply of key concepts of one's cultural or religious heritage). If a learning process exists solely to transmit and reinforce a cultural and theological heritage, it cannot empower the learner to think creatively, reflect independently and articulate transparently; it cannot ask the awkward questions for fear of what answers may be raised. The concept of problem solving does not easily fit into such a mould and yet learning by solving problems is a developing educational initiative, providing the possibility of moving beyond the traditional perspectives, received traditions and previously determined answers to those that can be determined in the context of mature thinking and critical objectivity. Education is thus not restricted to cognitive thinking but also embraces the development of sensitive understanding of issues and the possibility of shaping views and practices in a context that encourages careful thought and listening to and learning from others.

Pentecostals are exploring their own histories objectively. This sometimes results in painful discoveries but it demonstrates an integrity and readiness to be less polarized and polemical in maintaining one's distinctive Pentecostal views without the loss of objective discussion and analysis. Increasingly, study is dialogical and contextual – far removed from the programmed memorization of biblical texts to undergird doctrines felt to be important to the Pentecostal constituency concerned. Instead of seeking to indoctrinate students with preformed ideas or truths, colleges have become centres where learning is facilitated and enquiry is encouraged in a Spirit-inspired context where commitment to integrity, transparency and authenticity is prized. This is ever more important where Pentecostals are increasingly being confronted with an ever-changing culture and society. At the same time, whereas Pentecostal theology was taught using textbooks written by Evangelical authors, which in some areas (the role of women in ministry, supernatural phenomena, the inerrancy of the Bible) tended to gradually move Pentecostal students away from their traditional values, students are still guided in their exploration to consider other sources but also to recognize their own Pentecostal distinctives.[17]

College faculties are becoming more interested in offering education that meets the needs of people, including church leaders,[18] rather than simply following a programme of study that was relevant for previous eras, offered solutions for questions that were asked by a different audience and does not have an eye to the intended destination of the student.[19] They are becoming more aware of the need to determine syllabuses (including those that will be validated by external educational authorities) that reflect the needs of their students' future ministries rather than an unchanging framework of learning that lacks the opportunity to practically discover and experience God.[20] Theology is increasingly being applied and only taught if it is able to be applied. As such, since the 1950s and increasingly, the 1980s, Bible College curricula have increasingly been determined by Pentecostal faculties, even when the qualification receives university or governmental accreditation. Nevertheless, there are still challenges to tertiary education for Pentecostals that need to be addressed.

The Church and the Academy

Although this has been greatly reduced in some countries, some Pentecostals still take an anti-intellectual stance; Larbi acknowledges that African 'Pentecostals would like to hide behind closed doors and pray instead of presenting the gospel at the open market of ideas'.[21] Kennedy makes the valid point that 'Pentecostals have historically focused their attention on missionary projects rather than on establishing research institutions'[22] though the rise in the latter and the developing strengthening of the quality of the education being offered has seen significant growth in recent decades. At the same time Pentecostals have stood against an intellectualizing of their faith which would make it inaccessible to believers.

A symbiotic partnership needs to be strengthened between colleges and the church constituencies who send students there in order to maximize the learning process for all concerned, recognizing the different emphases and expectations stressed by each. The fear of being marginalized from the training of future leaders should cause all involved in Bible college education to reconsider what they are offering and its relevance. The church functions as a hermeneutical context for the learning and practice of the student. It can provide the college with the knowledge of whether it is providing what the Church needs; the academy must never forget that it is the servant of the Church (not its replacement) and that as such it must prove its value by helping the Church.[23] Syllabuses need to be envisaged that reflect the needs of society and the Church as well as students, rather than reflecting a model of the past that is assumed to be normative but is rarely tested. Both groups need to talk to each other with ears open wide. Thus, rather than the college being the only setting for learning, it is to be recognized that the better setting for prospective church leaders is the church community where mission can be developed in the appropriate context. A partnership between the local church and a residential college for intensive, dedicated sessions may be a suitable framework for ministry training and discipleship. Pentecostal denominations are already aware of this issue and are seeking to develop new models of training for pastors outside the Bible college framework. Interestingly, this has resulted in a proliferation of church-based colleges, established for a variety of reasons including a reluctance to send their best people to Bible college and a commitment to hands-on experience. A further significant reason is a commitment to leadership development through discipleship and impartation of vision from a successful leader. However, there are dangers of a multiplicity of Bible colleges being established, sometimes denomination or church based. Although these often have value and make education more widely available, they can also cater to the narrow beliefs of a given group and restrict wider engagement and learning with other believers. Nevertheless, rather than allow a division to develop, colleges ought to consider ways of supporting the learning and training processes that are taking place in the churches.

There are, however, important and valuable reasons for the existence of colleges and seminaries. They have value in 'promoting deep knowledge, careful research, and critical evaluation of thought' and do not by default restrict charismatic expression.[24]

The learning journey

Develop cross-cultural participation

There is a need for trained personnel and Pentecostal literature, especially in Majority world settings, as highlighted by Larbi.[25] Western colleges in particular can function as conduits and resources for providing educational development and training for leadership in settings where the infrastructure has not yet been established and finances are limited. They can also provide guidance with regard to the increasing need for accreditation by Bible colleges and, in particular, to ensure that a balance is maintained in the academic, applied and Pentecostal-nuanced components of the courses offered. At the same time, colleges in non-Western countries can provide invaluable cross-cultural experiences especially in areas where the Church is expanding rapidly.

Form a context of spiritual formation

From earliest times, some Pentecostals and others have spoken in disparaging terms of Bible schools, describing seminaries as 'cemeteries' and lampooning the titles of degrees earned or questioning their relevance or necessity. Although these comments have been exaggerations, nevertheless some colleges have lost their expectation of the supernatural, their spirituality has been less clearly Pentecostal and they have been less vocational or, at least, that has been the perception of outside observers.[26] This has been in part due to the personalities and gifts of those who have functioned in educational contexts but also due to the fact that spirituality is a personal discipline and that students often commence their studies with inadequate spiritual formation. However, where it has resulted in the students imbibing those features whilst in college, it has had a detrimental affect on the Church and the colleges. Instead, campuses should be the context for more proactive spiritual formation.[27]

There is a danger that theology can be taught in the absence of a spiritual framework. However, as Hudson notes, education and training for ministry cannot take place in the context of 'a disembodied spirituality'.[28] In this respect, it may be appropriate to re-visit the topic of 'the call of God', once the normal reason for people applying to Bible colleges in order to encourage the value of recognizing the role of God's guidance in the determining of one's destiny. The learning experience must feed into spirituality and transform character, to impart vision as well as learning.[29] This must start with the teachers themselves; McKinney encourages 'faculty to model a desire for continual spiritual renewal'.[30] It is often the lasting impact of the life of a teacher that affects students more than the information they have gained from the lectures. Also, the occasions where encounters with God are more likely, including corporate worship, need to be centralized in the curriculum.[31]

Provide a place for the spirit

In the pedagogical process, there needs to be an involvement of the Spirit and recognition that the learning journey is a holy one in which the Spirit is present as the great Teacher.[32] Anderson calls for a 'renewed focus on the role of the Holy Spirit in terms of learning and spiritual formation'.[33] However, Hudson warns, 'The ultimate irony is that the Spirit, that blows wherever he wills, has been codified, systematised and analysed',[34] whereas he also needs to be experienced. This need not be identified only in worship settings but by an awareness that he is speaking through the learning journey, the learners, the teachers, the questions, the probing analysis, and the silence. This calls for a particular type of learning environment. Teachers need to be Spirit-led learners and model Spirit-controlled lives, recognizing the Spirit's presence in the lives of their students, facilitating the students' exploration of the Spirit and giving the Spirit the opportunity to be a participatory guide and dialogue partner in the learning process. In the quest for rational theological models, it is essential that the mystery of God not be forgotten and that room be allowed for a dynamic interaction with him. Paul modelled this by walking with the Spirit, encouraging his readers to listen to the Spirit and expecting him to impact them experientially.

Motivate teachers to be ready to learn

Teachers must model that they are learners too. Theological educators in their attempts to explain must not become reductionistic to the point of losing a sense of mystery and wonder, and the readiness to recognize that the Bible does not answer all the questions addressed to it. Neither does it always provide clear and unambivolent guidance as to the validity of a given teaching. However, it does call for dialogue with it in the context of the Christian community and the presence of the Spirit. Land also comments on the ongoing need for 'an even deeper level theological work' to inspire 'unity, focus and renewed power' amongst Pentecostals.[35]

Identify the pre-college journey of the student

Teaching in Bible colleges is best determined after it has been appropriately contextualized in the life-settings of the students.[36] It is important to offer a learning environment for students that takes into consideration their previous experiences, spiritual journey and cultural distinctives.[37] To offer a form of theological education which follows the pattern of Western Bible colleges with a high stress on the cerebral may not be the most appropriate for the student. However, theology is not stagnant; it develops in a context. (Therefore, for example, exorcism could be explored differently with students from Africa to those from the UK because their worldviews, experience and praxis differ markedly.) The road travelled in the educational process needs to reflect the road already being travelled down by the student whilst enabling their level of consciousness to be raised to encompass vistas relevant to them though as yet not appreciated by them. Such education calls for a more individualistic, intensive and dynamic approach that may not be replicated in a pre-determined format which includes set reading and set notes and that assumes a static pedagogy within carefully defined limits. The best teacher responds to the prior experience of the learner or stimulates his/her curiosity, then goes to the subject and applies it to the experience of the learner or stimulates his/her curiosity.

Identify the requirements of the student

What are the academic, theological, spiritual, and socio-economic needs of the individual students? Educators need to be listeners as well as communicators, learners as well as teachers,[38] askers of questions and not just providers of answers, indulging in dialogue with fellow learners. They should not be functioning only in a teacher–pupil, expert–novice relationship but also in a Learner–learner relationship. The role of the teacher is not to be an expert who gathers together ever-increasing knowledge, some of which may be imparted to the listener; rather, they are to be facilitators. This needs a paradigm change away from learning how to teach, to learning more about learning in order to teach. This dynamic process – driven by the students' needs, not the content of the predetermined course – is difficult to be accommodated in a static framework of education with pre-set objectives. Training for ministry and discipleship is different to academic theological education. The theological issues in the lives and contexts of some students will be different to others. To try to meet their aspirations is a challenge but one that must be attended to carefully to facilitate a relevant and empowering learning journey. It means that one must offer different learning tracks, core and elective modules relevant to each student in an interdisciplinary format, as far as possible; new delivery systems need to be created for the diverse requirements of the learning communities in the Church. In the process, the student is incorporated as a partner in the learning journey in which the teacher is a guide and fellow traveller though not exclusively an authoritative determiner of the destination or the road to be travelled or the views or detours on the way. Without the institution of a contextual theological education, there is the danger that syllabuses will address issues that are absent from the lives of those who are taught from them.[39]

Identify the intended destination of the student

Before a learning journey is determined, it is necessary to deter-mine the intended outcome as anticipated by the learners. The problem with Western education is that it is all too often pre-determined before the student is even interviewed for a place on that course. Three concepts dominate Western university education, namely, *critical and evaluative* examination, *disciplined* research and *orderly* systems of learning offered in a framework of teaching and critical enquiry.[40] Though valid and laudable concepts, they may be less relevant for some vocations than for others. We need to be alert to the danger of offering a core curriculum that is static and not appropriately contextualized to the journey of our students thus far and their development thereafter. Unlike the classical educational model that moves from information to theory (often in a context of objective scholarship) and possibly to application, the model of 'paideia education' is better for future church leaders. The latter moves from 'source to personal appropriation of the source, from revealed wisdom to appropriation of revealed wisdom, in a way that is identity forming and personally transforming'.[41] If students are desirous of being mentored and discipled, a different mode of learning will need to be instituted than for someone who wishes a more academic route that incorporates enquiry, analysis and evaluation. If Bible colleges identify their goal as the creation of disciples, the framework of teaching will have to reflect the relevant paradigm; this may be reflected best in the life of Jesus but it differs from the normal education systems in ancient Graeco-Roman and modern Western Christian academies. Basing his findings on the educational milieu of the first century, Turnage makes a case for the Master–disciple model for theological education (rather than the scholar–pupil) as being the more appropriate for Christian education and as that which more closely reflected the practice of Jesus. He also recognizes the value of a more liberal education for the purposes of other students with different aspirations, as reflected in Paul's teaching model.[42]

Some colleges in non-Western settings have adopted Western models of education, syllabuses and (rationalist) philosophy. This has resulted in unhelpful frameworks for learning that has been, at times, harmful to the development of the Church.[43] Another danger is that Pentecostal colleges may seek scholarship at the expense of their core aspirations that may relate to other emphases such as church ministry, the training of leaders and the deepening of students' spirituality.[44]

Determine appropriate syllabuses

Once the outcome has been determined, the syllabus may be developed to ensure that the learning outcomes can be achieved. How relevant is our curriculum to the needs of the teacher, pastor, educationalist or student studying for the purposes of achieving a degree? The prospective pastor may be interested in answers concerning such issues as cohabitation, genetic engineering and gender distinctives while the scholar, teacher or evangelist will have a different agenda of interests and quests. What we must not be is too rooted in the educational *status quo*, such that we do not provide a dynamic response to contemporary questions. The question for teachers thus could increasingly become not so much 'how/what should I teach?' but 'how/what should they learn?'. That itself is based on the prior question, 'What do they need to learn?' (closely allied to, 'What do they want to learn?' that itself is associated with the question, 'What have they learned thus far?'). What one is considering here is a personal development plan that is partly based on pre-college development as well as post-college destination. This demands much more personal involvement but will result in a much better personal fulfilment of visions and vocations.

One aspect of such thinking would be to consider developing research centres dedicated to the present and also future needs of society that could be met by the Church.[45] Urban studies and church growth models would be two such issues for consideration incorporating the need for field studies.

Create good teaching models

The priorities of communication skills need to be explored. As well as identifying that which ought to be taught, the way it is communicated is also of paramount importance. The development of technology needs to be borne in mind in developing programmes relevant and accessible to more people. Local education is increasingly becoming global education.

Be enthusiastically interactive and praxis-based

Lebar[46] concludes that a student's 'growth is determined not by what he hears, but by what he does about what he hears'. Plueddeman[47] devised the rail fence model of education. As a rail fence is made up of two rails held together by fence posts, so also the educator must incorporate two metaphorical rails in his/her education methodology. The top rail equals truth; the lower one equals life and the role of the educator is to facilitate constant interaction between them both. Truth without life will result in deadness while life without truth will result in simplistic and short-lived experience. Harkness speaks of the need of having a 'praxiological agenda'.[48] There is a great danger that education has spawned a new breed of people ... professional listeners. Even this is speculative if the maxim that a lecturer is a person who speaks in someone else's sleep is correct. It is estimated that at any one time, only 26 per cent of an audience is actively listening to a preacher; are lecturers likely to achieve better results? If the lecture involves people being talked at, the lecturer won't be listened to. Teaching must involve interchange, taking into consideration the contexts of those present.

Judy was just six years old; she loved playing school. 'Why not play Sunday school?', asked her mother. 'No', said Judy, 'All we do there is sit and listen. We don't learn anything'. If lectures involve sitting and listening, we are living in a dream world if we presume that students are always listening, let alone learning. Lectures must be much more than simply spoken books; in fact, if a lecture simply repeats information that is already included in a multiplicity of books, it is surely advisable and cheaper to buy the books.

Jesus taught wisdom (and how to develop it) more than he imparted information (and how to enlarge it); 'how' more than 'what'; 'why' more than 'when'; who you are more than what you know; who you can become more than what you can retain. Closely allied to the content of his teaching was the context of his teaching. The content was imparted in the context of praxis and practising; less knowledge and more know-how; less information and more application, less intensive data presentation and more inspiration and transformation; no notes and handouts but hands-on-experience; less cerebral and more personal development; less intellectual and more intuitive; not just the impartation of information but the directing of self-activity; giving what was needed not what was interesting or what might be useful; pragmatic not idealistic; but also not only giving what he thought the person ought to know but what the person was capable of receiving (Mk. 4:33; Jn. 16:12). Jesus is the best paradigm of brilliant pedagogy.

Groome comments on the two main terms used to describe Jewish teaching methodology. Both (*yârâh, yāda*) may be used to define the concepts of teaching and informing others. However, the latter carries with it the notion of learning via experiential encounter with a given subject.[49] Rice, building on these perspectives, suggests Pentecostal educators should encapsulate their teaching in experiential and dynamic forms.[50] Lectures are usually ineffective in changing attitudes unless discussion is involved. Speaking can be a good means of communicating as long as it is multi-dimensional in presentation. Alexander[51] speaks of the role of the 'living teacher' as being crucial in the early Church. The written and spoken word will always be a poor second to the living voice that is enthusiastic, interactive and transformational. Kierkegaard (1813–55) said, 'If God held all truth in (the) right hand, and in (the) left hand held the lifelong pursuit of it, (God) would choose the left hand'. An enthusiastic pursuit of the exploration of God is crucial to the learning journey.

If students are to be trained to be 'out there', they need to be 'out there' when they are being trained. The academic model is not the best one for discipleship/pastoral training; degrees do not necessarily make better disciples; too often they simply bestow doctrine; degrees can lead to rationalism not to radicalism, learning rather than learned behaviour, libraries not lifestyles. The model used by Jesus for ministry and discipleship training was a three-year, intensive, on-the-job training with a high reliance on example, character development and practice, whilst being rooted in community; in a word, discipleship.

Teach engagingly

Jesus was funny (hyperbole – Mt. 7:3–5). He was provocative and made them think (overstatement – Mt. 5:29–30; riddles – Mk. 14:58). He used clever speech (pun – Mt. 23:24). He used language that was relevant to his audience (*a fortiori* – Mt. 6:28–30). He used picture language (similes – Mt. 10:16; metaphors – Mt. 5:13–16; proverbs – Mt. 6:21). He taught by actions (eating at Zacchaeus' home expressed his determination to eat with the marginalized (Lk. 19:1–7)).[52] He engaged in interactive discourse that was both practical and relevant, because he contextualized it (Mk. 3:1–4). He was person-centred, challenging people to move from passivity to action, transformed by his teaching, prepared for community service. He taught, expecting a decision, choosing not to speak simply theologically but also practically (thus, he did not offer facts about demons but demonstrated by action what they were and how to deal with them).

Adapt to the audience

The crowds, the disciples, the opposition, the enquirers – each were dealt with differently. Instead of a systematized theology, his theology was life based. Thus, in a situation of fear aroused by a storm, he taught about trust (Mt. 8:23–27). When they felt alone and insecure, he taught them about the role of the Spirit as helper (Jn. 14:1–17). He sparred with Nicodemus (Jn. 3:1–21) in a highly articulate, complicated and verbally stylish question and answer session that probably would have been too sophisticated for the disciples. In the following narrative (4:1–26), Jesus was different. Here, he aroused a woman's curiosity, displayed supernatural knowledge about her and led her to himself through pictures of water and worship. To the Pharisees and their scribes, he offered acted dramas to help them in their voyage of discovery. Mark, for example, provides the journey that Jesus charts for them. Thus, he eats with the embarrassing people who sin as a way of life, to demonstrate that he has the authority to eat with whoever he chooses (2:15–17); he eats, when others are fasting, to demonstrate his authority to decide the rules concerning fasting (2:17–22); he walks through a grainfield and reveals his authority to decide what is acceptable practice on the Sabbath (2:23–28). Unfortunately, although the pedagogy was perfect, the lessons were missed and the students tried to kill their teacher.

Teach appropriately

He taught his disciples in bite-sized morsels of teaching, easily digestible, but also provided learning opportunities in the context of continuous mission activity. He didn't teach in a vacuum; he only taught that which they needed to know at any given moment and he presented it often in snack form, and, when they were full, the feeding stopped. Teaching in college settings is often determined by the length of module, credit rating and length of lecture; it is a constant challenge to ensure that students receive that which is right for them. Jesus' teaching was relational, generally informal and reciprocal.[53] The question to be addressed consistently is how one can apply aspects of his pedagogy to current teaching styles.

Conclusion

At the *Teaching Research and Development Network* annual symposium on 15 May 2002, at the University of Manchester, the keynote speaker was Professor Charles Engel. His underlying proposition was, 'the twenty-first century will witness an escalation in the frequency and gravity of changes that will affect society worldwide'. Change is here to stay and educationalists must be prepared to embrace this fact, including the challenges and the potential. How we deal with it will define our future. The evidence of how successful we may be in this regard will be identified by how much we have been willing to change ourselves before we seek to change those who come and learn with us and from us.

John Amos Comenius (1592–1670) was a Christian educator (the first who popularized pictures in teaching) who has been described as the first modern educator. He lived much of his life in poverty though he was highly respected in Europe. Sweden asked him to reform their schools; England asked him to set up a research college. His major work was entitled *The Great Didactic*. On the title page, he wrote his objective: 'To seek to find a method of instruction, by which teachers may teach less, but learners may learn more.' This must always be our aim.

Bibliography

Alexander, L., 'The Living Voice. Skepticism towards the Written Word in Early Christian and in Graeco-Roman Texts' in Clines, D.J.A., S.E. Fowl, S.E. Porter (eds.), *The Bible in Three Dimensions: Essays in Celebration of Forty Years of Biblical Studies in the University of Sheffield* (Sheffield: Sheffield Academic, 1990).

Alvarez, M., 'Distinctives of Pentecostal Education', *AJPS* 3.2 (2000).

Anderson, A., 'The "Fury and Wonder": Pentecostal-Charismatic Spirituality in Theological Education', *Pneuma* 23.2 (2001).

Anderson, B.A., 'Missional Orientation and its Implications for Pentecostal Theological Education', *JEPTA* 26.2 (2000).

Ayuk, A.A., 'Portrait of a Nigerian Pentecostal Missionary', *AJPS* 8.1 (2005).

Becker, M., 'A Tenet under Examination: Reflections on the Pentecostal Hermeneutical Approach', *JEPTA* 24 (2004).

Bowdle, D.N., 'Informed Pentecostalism: An Alternative Paradigm' in *The Spirit and the Mind. Essays in Informed Pentecostalism. To honor Dr. Donald Bowdle. Presented on his 65th Birthday,* edited by T.L. Cross and E.B. Powery (Lanham, MD: University Press of America, 2000).

Brenkus, J., 'A Historical and Theological Analysis of the Pentecostal Church in the Czech and Slovak Republics', *JEPTA* 20 (2000).

Bundy, D.D., 'Historical and Theological Analysis of the Pentecostal Church in Norway', *JEPTA* 20 (2000).

Bundy, D.D., 'Historical Perspectives on the Development of the European Pentecostal Theological Association,' *Pneuma: The Journal of the Society for Pentecostal Studies* 2:2 (Fall, 1980).

Castleberry, J.L., 'Pentecostal Seminaries are Essential to the Future Health of the Church', *Pneuma* 26.2 (2004).

Collinson S., 'Making Disciples: An Educational Strategy for Use Beyond the Time of Jesus', *Journal of Christian Education* 43.3 (2000).

Daniels, D., 'Live so can use me anytime, Lord, anywhere (*sic*): Theological Education in the Church of God in Christ, 1970–1997', *AJPS* 3.2 (2000).

Dovre, P.J. (ed.), *The Future of Religious Colleges* (Grand Rapids, MI: Eerdmans, 2002).

Dresselhaus, R., 'What Can the Academy do for the Church?', *AJPS* 3.2 (2000).

Espinosa, G., 'Bible Institutes, Spanish-speaking' in Burgess, S.M., Van der Maas, E.M. (eds.), *The New International Dictionary of Pentecostal and Charismatic Movements* (Grand Rapids, MI: Zondervan, 2002).

Farley, E., *Theologia: The Fragmentation and Unity of Theological Education* (Philadelphia, PA: Fortress, 1983).

—, *The Fragility of Knowledge* (Philadelphia, PA: Fortress, 1988).

Ferris, R.W. (ed.), *Renewal in Theological Education: Strategies for Change* (Billy Graham Center: Wheaton College, 1990).

Flattery, G.M., 'Accreditation of Pentecostal Colleges in Europe' (EPTA Conference paper, Brussels, 1980).

Groome, T.H., *Christian Religious Education: Sharing Our Story and Vision* (San Francisco, CA: Jossey-Bass, 1980).

Harkness, A.G., 'De-schooling the Theological Seminary: An Appropriate Paradigm for Effective Ministerial Formation', *Teaching Theology and Religion* 4.3 (2001).

Hathaway, M.R., 'Trends in Ministerial Training' (EPTA Conference paper, Brussels, 1980).

Hedlund, R.E., 'Critique of Pentecostal Mission by a Friendly Evangelical', *AJPS* 8.1 (2005).

Hittenberger, J.S., 'Toward a Pentecostal Philosophy of Education', *Pneuma*, 23.2 (Fall 2001).

—, 'Globalization, "Marketization", and the Mission of Pentecostal Higher Education in Africa', *Pneuma* 26.2 (2004).

Hollenweger, W.J., 'Pentecostalism and Academic Theology: From Confrontation to Cooperation', *Epta Bulletin*, 11. 1 & 2 (1992).

—, 'The Challenge of Reconciliation', *JEPTA* 19 (1999).

Hudson, D.N., 'It's not what we do: it's the way we do it. Uncomfortable thoughts for a lecturer in a residential Bible College at the turn of the century', *JEPTA* 23 (2003).

Hunter, H.D., 'International Pentecostal-Charismatic Scholarly Associations' in Burgess, S.M., and E.M. Van der Maas (eds.), *The New International Dictionary of Pentecostal and Charismatic Movements* (Grand Rapids, MI: Zondervan, 2002).

Jacobsen, D., 'Knowing the Doctrine of Pentecostals: The Scholastic Theology of the Assemblies of God, 1930–1955' in Bays, D., 'The Protestant Missionary Establishment and the Pentecostal Movement' in Blumhofer, E.L, R.P. Spittler and G.A. Wacker (eds.), *Pentecostal Currents in American Protestantism* (Urbana, IL: University of Illinois Press, 1999).

Johns, C.B., 'The Meaning of Pentecost for Theological Education', *Ministerial Formation* 87.

—, *Pentecostal Formation: A Pedagogy Among the Oppressed* (Sheffield: Sheffield Academic Press, 1993).

Jurgensen, H., 'Theological Trends and our Pentecostal Commitments' (EPTA Conference paper, Brussels, 1980).

Kay, W.K., 'Pentecostal Education', *Journal of Beliefs and Values* 25.2 (2004).

—, 'Sociology of British Pentecostal and Charismatic Movements' in Burgess, S.M., Van der Maas, E.M. (eds.), *The New International Dictionary of Pentecostal and Charismatic Movements* (Grand Rapids, MI: Zondervan, 2002).

Kelsey, D.H., *Between Athens and Berlin: The Theological Education Debate* (Grand Rapids MI: Eerdmans 1993).

Kennedy, J.R., 'Anti-Intellectualism' in *Encyclopedia of Pentecostal and Charismatic Christianity* (ed.) Burgess, S. (London: Routledge, 2006).

Land, S., *Pentecostal Spirituality: A Passion for the Kingdom* (Sheffield: Sheffield Academic Press, 1993).

Larbi, E.K., *Pentecostalism: The Eddies of Ghanaian Christianity* (Accra: Centre for Pentecostal and Charismatic Studies, 2001).

Lebar, L., Plueddemann, J., *Education that is Christian* (Wheaton, IL: Victor, 1989).

Lee, E., 'What the Academy needs from the Church', *AJPS* 3.2 (July 2000).

Ma, W., 'Biblical Studies in the Pentecostal Tradition: Yesterday, Today, and Tomorrow' in Dempster, M.W., B.D. Klaus and D. Petersen (eds.), *The Globalization of Pentecostalism: A Religion Made to Travel* (Oxford: Regnum, 1999).

Maachia, F.D., 'The Struggle for Global Witness: Shifting Paradigms in Pentecostal Theology' in Dempster, M.W., B.D. Klaus and D. Petersen (eds.), *The Globalization of Pentecostalism: A Religion Made to Travel* (Oxford: Regnum, 1999).

McClung, L.G., 'Salvation Shock Troops' in Smith, H.B. (ed.), *Pentecostals from the Inside Out* (Wheaton, IL: Victory, 1990).

McKinney, E.L., 'Some Spiritual Aspects of Pentecostal Education: A Personal Journey', *AJPS* 3.2 (2000).

Nañez, R.M., *Full Gospel, Fractured Minds? A Call to Use God's Gift of the Intellect* (Grand Rapids, MI: Eerdmans, 2005).

Pagaialii, T., 'The Pentecostal Movement of Samoa: Reaching the Uttermost', *AJPS* 7.1 (2004).

Palmer, M., 'Orienting our Lives: The Importance of a Liberal Education for Pentecostals in the Twenty First Century', *Pneuma* 23.2 (2001).

Pandrea, R., 'A Historical and Theological Analysis of the Pentecostal Church in Romania', *JEPTA* 21 (2001).

Petts, D., 'Classroom Methods and Theological Education' (EPTA Conference paper, Brussels, 1980).

Plueddemann, J., 'The Real Disease of the Sunday School: Rail Fence Analogy for Curriculum Design', *Evangelical Missions Quarterly* 8.2 (1972).

Renstorf, K.H., *'manthanō', Theological Dictionary of the New Testament Vols 1–10* (eds.) Kittel, G., Friedrich, G., (transl) Bromiley, G. (Grand Rapids, MI: Eerdmans, 1964–76).

Rice, M.L., 'Pneumatic Experience as Teaching Methodology in Pentecostal Tradition', *AJPS* 5.2 (2002).

Robeck, C.M. Jr., 'Seminaries and Graduate Schools' in Burgess, S.M., Van der Maas, E.M. (eds.), *The New International Dictionary of Pentecostal and Charismatic Movements* (Grand Rapids, MI: Zondervan, 2002).

Ruthven, J., 'Are Pentecostal Seminaries a Good Idea?', *Pneuma* 26.2 (2004).

Sepúlveda, J., 'The Challenge for Theological Education from a Pentecostal Standpoint', *Ministerial Formation* 87 (1999).

Stevens, R.P., 'Marketing the Faith – A Reflection on the Importing and Exporting of Western Theological Education', *Crux* 38.2 (1992).

Sun, B., 'Assemblies of God Theological Education in Asia Pacific: A Reflection', *AJPS* 3.2 (2000).

Tarr, D., 'Transcendence, Immanence, and the Emerging Pentecostal Academy' in Ma, W., Menzies, R.P. (eds.), *Pentecostalism in Context. Essays in Honour of William W. Menzies* (Sheffield: Sheffield Academic Press, 1997).

Thomas, J.C., 'Pentecostal Explorations of the New Testament: Teaching New Testament Introduction in a Pentecostal Seminary', *JPT* 11.1 (2002).

Turnage, M., 'The Early Church and the Axis of History and Pentecostalism facing the 21st Century: Some Reflections', *JEPTA* 23 (2003).

Wanak, L., 'Theological Education and the Role of Teachers in the 21st century: A Look at the Asia Pacific Region', *Journal of Asian Mission* 2.1 (2000).

Wenk, M., 'Do we need a distinct European Pentecostal/Charismatic approach to theological education', *JEPTA* 23 (2003).

Wilson, L.F., 'Bible Institutes, Colleges, Universities' in Burgess, S.M., Van der Maas, E.M. (eds.), *The New International Dictionary of Pentecostal and Charismatic Movements* (Grand Rapids, MI: Zondervan, 2002).

Yung, H., 'Critical Issues Facing Theological Education in Asia', *Transformation* (Oct–Dec. 1995).

Notes

1 McClung, L.G., 'Salvation Shock Troops' in Smith, H.B. (ed.), *Pentecostals from the Inside Out* (Wheaton, IL: Victory, 1990), 86 (81–90).

2 Maachia, F.D., 'The Struggle for Global Witness: Shifting Paradigms in Pentecostal Theology' in Dempster, M.W., B.D. Klaus and D. Petersen (eds.), *The Globalization of Pentecostalism: A Religion Made to Travel* (Oxford: Regnum, 1999), 9 (8–29).

3 Wilson, L.F., 'Bible Institutes, Colleges, Universities' in Burgess, S.M., Van der Maas, E.M. (eds.), *The New International Dictionary of Pentecostal and Charismatic Movements* (Grand Rapids, MI: Zondervan, 2002), 373 (372–80).

4 Palmer, M., 'Orienting our Lives: The Importance of a Liberal Education for Pentecostals in the Twenty First Century', *Pneuma* 23.2 (2001), 204–6.

5 Kay, W.K., 'Sociology of British Pentecostal and Charismatic Movements' in Burgess, S.M., Van der Maas, E.M. (eds.), *The New International Dictionary of Pentecostal and Charismatic Movements* (Grand Rapids, MI: Zondervan, 2002), 1081 (1080–83).

6 Warrington, K., 'Would Jesus have sent his disciples to Bible College?', *JEPTA* 23 (2003), 30–44; Tarr, D., 'Transcendence, Immanence, and the Emerging Pentecostal Academy' in Ma, W., Menzies, R.P. (eds.), *Pentecostalism in Context: Essays in Honour of William W. Menzies* (Sheffield: Sheffield Academic Press, 1997), 195–222; Robeck, C.M. Jr., 'Seminaries and Graduate Schools' in Burgess, S.M., Van der Maas, E.M. (eds.), *The New International Dictionary of Pentecostal and Charismatic Movements* (Grand Rapids, MI: Zondervan, 2002), 1045–50; Ferris, R.W. (ed.), *Renewal in Theological Education: Strategies for Change* (Billy Graham Center: Wheaton College, 1990); Lee, E., 'What

the Academy needs from the Church', *AJPS,* 3.2 (July 2000); 311–18; Hittenberger, J.S., 'Toward a Pentecostal Philosophy of Education', *Pneuma,* 23.2 (Fall 2001) 217–44; Dovre, P.J. (ed.), *The Future of Religious Colleges* (Grand Rapids, MI: Eerdmans, 2002); Johns, C.B., *Pentecostal Formation: A Pedagogy Among the Oppressed* (Sheffield: Sheffield Academic Press, 1993), 111–40; Kay, W.K., 'Pentecostal Education', *Journal of Beliefs and Values* 25.2 (2004), 229–39; Sepúlveda, J., 'The Challenge for Theological Education from a Pentecostal Standpoint', *Ministerial Formation* 87 (1999), 29–34.

[7] Wilson, 'Bible …', 375–9; Espinosa, G., 'Bible Institutes, Spanish-speaking' in Burgess, S.M., Van der Maas, E.M. (eds.), *The New International Dictionary of Pentecostal and Charismatic Movements* (Grand Rapids, MI: Zondervan, 2002), 380–1; Hunter, H.D., 'International Pentecostal-Charismatic Scholarly Associations' in Burgess, S.M., Van der Maas, E.M. (eds.), *The New International Dictionary of Pentecostal and Charismatic Movements* (Grand Rapids, MI: Zondervan, 2002), 795–7; Hedlund, R.E., 'Critique of Pentecostal Mission by a Friendly Evangelical', *AJPS* 8.1 (2005), 83–4 (67–94); Sun, B., 'Assemblies of God Theological Education in Asia Pacific: A Reflection', *AJPS* 3.2 (2000), 232–41; Daniels, D., 'Live so can use me anytime, Lord, anywhere (*sic*): Theological Education in the Church of God in Christ, 1970–1997', *AJPS* 3.2 (2000), 295–310; Hittenberger, J.S., 'Globalization, 'Marketization', and the Mission of Pentecostal Higher Education in Africa', *Pneuma* 26.2 (2004), 182–215.

[8] Sepúlveda, J., 'The Challenge for Theological Education from a Pentecostal Standpoint', *Ministerial Formation* 87 (1999), 29–34 (29); Wilson, 'Bible …', 374.

[9] Hedlund, 'Critique …', 89.

[10] Ayuk, A.A., 'Portrait of a Nigerian Pentecostal Missionary', *AJPS* 8.1 (2005), 133–6 (117–141).

[11] Pagaialii, T., 'The Pentecostal Movement of Samoa: Reaching the Uttermost', *AJPS* 7.1 (2004), 273–5 (265–279).

[12] Bowdle, D.N., 'Informed Pentecostalism: An Alternative Paradigm' in *The Spirit and the Mind: Essays in Informed Pentecostalism. To honor Dr. Donald Bowdle. Presented on his 65th Birthday,* (ed.) Cross, T.L., Powery, E.B. (Lanham, MD: University Press of America, 2000) 12, 13–15 (9–19); Bundy notes that in early Pentecostalism in Norway, there was much evidence of theological dialogue, even of controversial issues (Bundy, D.D., 'Historical and Theological Analysis of the Pentecostal Church in Norway', *JEPTA* 20 (2000), 82 (66–92).

[13] Pandrea, R., 'A Historical and Theological Analysis of the Pentecostal Church in Romania', *JEPTA* 21 (2001), 128–9 (109–35).

[14] Ma, W., 'Biblical Studies in the Pentecostal Tradition: Yesterday, Today, and Tomorrow' in Dempster, M.W., B.D. Klaus and D. Petersen (eds.), *The Globalization of Pentecostalism: A Religion Made to Travel* (Oxford: Regnum, 1999), 57–64 (52–69); Bowdle, 'Informed …', 9–10; Brenkus, J., 'A Historical and Theological Analysis of the Pentecostal Church in the Czech and Slovak Republics', *JEPTA* 20 (2000) 63 (49–65); Jacobsen, D., 'Knowing the Doctrine of Pentecostals: The Scholastic Theology of the Assemblies of God, 1930–1955' in Bays, D., 'The Protestant Missionary Establishment and the Pentecostal Movement' in Blumhofer, E.L, R.P. Spittler and G.A. Wacker (eds.), *Pentecostal Currents in American Protestantism* (Urbana, IL: University of Illinois Press, 1999), 90–107.

[15] Journals, e.g. *Journal of Pentecostal Theology, Journal of the European Pentecostal Theological Association, Asian Journal of Pentecostal Studies, Pneuma*; Societies, e.g. *The Society of Pentecostal Studies, European Pentecostal Theological Association, European Pentecostal Charismatic Research Association*; Hollenweger, W.J., 'The Challenge of Reconciliation', *JEPTA* 19 (1999), 8–12; Bundy, D.D., 'Historical Perspectives on the Development of the European Pentecostal Theological Association,' *Pneuma: The Journal of the Society for Pentecostal Studies* 2:2 (Fall, 1980), 15–25.

[16] Hollenweger, W.J., 'Pentecostalism and Academic Theology: From Confrontation to Cooperation', *Epta Bulletin* 11. 1 & 2 (1992), 42–9; Nañez, R.M., *Full Gospel, Fractured Minds? A Call to Use God's Gift of the Intellect* (Grand Rapids, MI: Eerdmans, 2005).

[17] Thomas, J.C., 'Pentecostal Explorations of the New Testament: Teaching New Testament Introduction in a Pentecostal Seminary', *JPT* 11.1 (2002), 120–9.

[18] Hathaway, M.R., 'Trends in Ministerial Training' (EPTA Conference paper, Brussels, 1980), 16–27.

[19] Jurgensen, H., 'Theological Trends and our Pentecostal Commitments' (EPTA Conference paper, Brussels, 1980), 28–49.

[20] Macchia, 'The Struggle …', p. 9; Flattery, G.M., 'Accreditation of Pentecostal Colleges in Europe' (EPTA Conference paper, Brussels, 1980); Petts, D., 'Classroom Methods and Theological Education' (EPTA Conference paper, Brussels, 1980), 50–5.

[21] Larbi, E.K., *Pentecostalism: The Eddies of Ghanaian Christianity* (Accra: Centre for Pentecostal and Charismatic Studies, 2001), 447

[22] Kennedy, J.R., 'Anti-Intellectualism' in *Encyclopedia of Pentecostal and Charismatic Christianity* (ed.) Burgess, S. (London: Routledge, 2006), 35–9.

23 Dresselhaus, R., 'What Can the Academy do for the Church?', *AJPS* 3.2 (2000), 319–23.

24 Castleberry, J.L., 'Pentecostal Seminaries are Essential to the Future Health of the Church', *Pneuma* 26.2 (2004), 346–54 (351).

25 Larbi, *Pentecostalism . . .* , 446–8.

26 Tarr, D., 'Transcendence, Immanence, and the Emerging Pentecostal Academy' in Ma, W., Menzies, R.P. (eds.), *Pentecostalism in Context. Essays in Honour of William W. Menzies* (Sheffield: Sheffield Academic Press, 1997) 206–7, 211–12 (195–222).

27 Wenk, M., 'Do we need a distinct European Pentecostal/Charismatic approach to theological education' *JEPTA* 23 (2003), 61–2 (58–71).

28 Hudson, D.N., 'It's not what we do: it's the way we do it. Uncomfortable thoughts for a lecturer in a residential Bible College at the turn of the century', *JEPTA* 23 (2003), 45–57.

29 McKinney, E.L., 'Some Spiritual Aspects of Pentecostal Education: A Personal Journey', *AJPS* 3.2 (2000), 253–79; Alvarez, M., 'Distinctives of Pentecostal Education', *AJPS* 3.2 (2000), 282–93.

30 McKinney, 'Some . . .', 262.

31 Hittenberger, J.S., 'Toward a Pentecostal Philosophy of Education', *Pneuma* 23.2 (2001), 223.

32 Johns, C.B., 'The Meaning of Pentecost for Theological Education', *Ministerial Formation* 87 (1999). 42–7.

33 Anderson, B.A., 'Missional Orientation and its Implications for Pentecostal Theological Education', *JEPTA* 26.2 (2000), 145 (134–136); Hittenberger, J.S., 'Toward a Pentecostal Philosophy of Education', *Pneuma* 23.2 (Fall 2001), 217–44.

34 Hudson, 'It's not what we do . . .', 49.

35 Land, S., *Pentecostal Spirituality: A Passion for the Kingdom* (Sheffield: Sheffield Academic Press, 1993), 191.

36 Anderson, A., 'The 'Fury and Wonder'? Pentecostal-Charismatic Spirituality in Theological Education', *Pneuma* 23.2 (2001) 287–302; Wanak, L., 'Theological Education and the Role of Teachers in the 21st Century: A Look at the Asia Pacific Region', *Journal of Asian Mission* 2.1 (2000), 11 (3–24)

37 Warrington, 'Would . . .', 39–41.

38 Cf. Harkness, A.G., 'De-schooling the Theological Seminary: An Appropriate Paradigm for Effective Ministerial Formation', *Teaching Theology and Religion* 4.3 (2001), 150–1 (141–54).

39 Anderson, A., 'The 'Fury and Wonder': Pentecostal-Charismatic Spirituality in Theological Education', *Pneuma* 23.2 (2001), 287–302.

40 Kelsey, D.H., *Between Athens and Berlin: The Theological Education Debate* (Grand Rapids, MI: Eerdmans, 1993), 13; Farley, E., *The Fragility of Knowledge* (Philadelphia, PA: Fortress, 1988), 4–5.

41 Kelsey, *Between Athens...*, 19–20; Farley, E., *Theologia: The Fragmentation and Unity of Theological Education* (Philadelphia, PA: Fortress, 1983).

42 Turnage, M., 'The Early Church and the Axis of History and Pentecostalism facing the 21st Century: Some Reflections', *JEPTA* 23 (2003), 4–29.

43 Yung, H., 'Critical Issues Facing Theological Education in Asia', *Transformation* (Oct–Dec. 1995), 1 (1–6).

44 Ruthven, J., 'Are Pentecostal Seminaries a Good Idea?', *Pneuma* 26.2 (2004), 339–45.

45 Sun, B., 'Assemblies of God Theological Education in Asia Pacific: A Reflection', *AJPS* 3.2 (2000), 244.

46 Lebar, L., Plueddemann, J., *Education that is Christian* (Wheaton, IL: Victor, 1989), 166.

47 Plueddemann, J., 'The Real Disease of the Sunday School: Rail Fence Analogy for Curriculum Design', *Evangelical Missions Quarterly* 8.2 (1972), 88–92.

48 Harkness, 'De-schooling ...', 152.

49 Groome, T.H., *Christian Religious Education: Sharing Our Story and Vision* (San Francisco, CA: Jossey-Bass, 1980), 139–51; Becker, M., 'A Tenet under Examination: Reflections on the Pentecostal Hermeneutical Approach', *JEPTA* 24 (2004), 38–9 (30–48).

50 Rice, M.L., 'Pneumatic Experience as Teaching Methodology in Pentecostal Tradition', *AJPS* 5.2 (2002), 295–6 (289–312).

51 Alexander, L., 'The Living Voice. Skepticism towards the Written Word in Early Christian and in Graeco-Roman Texts' in Clines, D.J.A., S.E. Fowl, S.E. Porter (eds.), *The Bible in three Dimensions: Essays in Celebration of Forty Years of Biblical Studies in the University of Sheffield* (Sheffield: Sheffield Academic, 1990), 244 (221–47).

52 See also Renstorf, K.H., *manthanō, Theological Dictionary of the New Testament Vols 1–10* (eds.) Kittel, G., Friedrich, G. (transl) Bromiley, G. (Grand Rapids, MI: Eerdmans, 1964–76), vol. 4., 435; Gerhardsson, B., *Memory and Manuscript: Oral Tradition and Written Transmission in Rabbinic Judaism and Early Christianity*, Lund (1964), 181–7.

53 See further Collinson S., 'Making Disciples: An Educational Strategy for Use Beyond the Time of Jesus', *Journal of Christian Education* 43.3 (2000) 15–16 (7–18); Stevens, R.P., 'Marketing the Faith – A Reflection on the Importing and Exporting of Western Theological Education', *Crux* 38.2 (1992), 17 (6–18).

10

Repairing the Breach:[1] Developing a Spirituality for Leadership Today

Canon Anne Dyer

Changing times, changing spiritualites?

Do the changing times that we live in, in which the churches are struggling to respond and adapt to contemporary challenges in mission, require leaders to have spiritualities that are markedly different from their predecessors? Will the search for new pathways require new ways of praying and living, so that leaders will be able to find the path and walk in it? What kind of habits of life, network of relationships, and accountability structures will sustain a leadership that is healthy and life-giving to the churches and stands the tests of this time? In the area of Christian spirituality there is much to suggest that something new is required, but we need to consider this carefully.

First of all we must consider what a 'spirituality' is. I understand it as those things that provide the foundations for Christian life and service. Our spiritual life is that which keeps us 'on the way' with Jesus, it is the bedrock of discipleship. The many elements include our life of prayer and worship; personal and corporate, our participation in the community of believers; most especially at the Lord's Supper, the reading and study of Scripture, and the practice of hospitality, care for the poor and forgiveness. It also includes our openness to scrutiny and our accountability to others. It includes the love of our enemies, the turning of our cheeks towards those who hurt us and a preparedness to 'travel' on behalf of another who is not loved by us and does not love us in return. All of these things have been part of the Christian life from the Church's beginnings in the group gathered around Jesus. In one form or another these practices have been passed on from one generation to the next. Our question is this: what form should these things take today if leaders, especially younger leaders, are to be faithful as they make their journey 'on the way' in times that are not easy?

From all that has been written about life at the beginning of the twenty-first century it might seem that the challenge of change is something that is unique to the present generations. We know that this is not the case. Throughout the modern period, from the time of the Black Death and the rise of humanism that led to a long and sustained period of renaissance and reformation, change has been rapid and escalating. One mark of this change has been that the wisdom of one generation fails the next because the circumstances of life have changed so much. This failure seems very acute at the beginning of this century where younger leaders, inside and outside the churches, are inheriting a world marked by rapid technological innovation and instant global communication, increasing independence of living, a growing number of poor people, together with excluded groups that include significant numbers of children. All these, together with an inherited disregard for the environment, are the markers of challenging times of great change. How can the lives and spiritualities of the generations that are passing on such a world have anything to teach younger leaders?

And even if our world stopped changing, if some part of it was steady and safe and reliably the same (which is what many would like the Church to be), the people that make up the churches would themselves be constantly changing through the processes of ageing. From childhood and adolescence through to the mid-life challenges of being 50 (and the average age of a church leader in Britain is 54) and beyond, we age and experience life events that give us very different views of or 'takes' on our world. How we see, think, relate and pray changes with time – or it does if we are healthy and living in a manner that is open to God and to the world. And so we notice that there are a number of key times in human lives when faith is found, adapted or lost altogether. Children that were happy to accept the faith of their parents drift away in their teens, while many others find faith for the first time in the opening, questioning years of their late teens and early 20s. Some come to faith around the time of the challenge of mature adult relationships and responsibilities, particularly in marriage or in parenting, while others drift away from church and faith during the mid-life challenges of caring for elderly parents. The death of parents, resonating with mid-life questions about the purpose of one's life (is it generative or stagnant?), can again lead to a crisis through which people find or lose faith. So, the primary personal issues for those over 50, that is for those that lead the denominations (traditional or new), are not those for most young leaders. This difference in life-stage brings a dissonance that results in many of the tensions seen in the selection, training and deployment of younger leaders, especially for those that want to challenge the content or value of older patterns of church. More than anything young leaders who are healthily inhabiting their own life-stage have passion for the gospel, passion that can run away into the sand as they encounter the questioning, thoughtful spirituality of those who are healthily inhabiting mid-life.

If this was not enough change there is more. Maybe the most significant change when comparing the make-up of the leaders of churches today with the leadership, say, in the 1960s and 1970s (that is the time when today's gate-keeper generation was being formed), is that there are significant numbers of women emerging as leaders in their own right. This development challenges the assumptions surrounding the shape of life and spirituality of the inherited model of male leadership. Today's feminized churches (that is female and family friendly, configured around family life rather than work life) have emerged under male leadership. More women than men attend or participate in church, and yet the leadership, control and gate-keeping on major decisions has been done by men. The leadership culture is strongly masculine, and the values of male worlds easily imported without notice. This is so much a given, that it will seem to many that there is no masculine culture in church leadership, this is just how church is. However, it can be a far from comfortable environment for women, especially when caught in some event where the male leaders present are giving strong indications that they think size matters, and are busy working out who in the room is the top dog. And as soon as God's blessing is associated with size or success, and leadership comes to be about power and control, then both the women and men present might feel the Church has slipped a long way from the lived spirituality of those that followed Jesus on the way. When these things become the marks of a prayer meeting, or a time of fellowship, then there might be a significant inner movement among the more marginal people present (often women) to reject this model of spirituality and find another way.

Leadership and prayer

In the evangelical tradition there has always been a strong emphasis on personal prayer. Sometimes called the 'quiet time', it was 'a given' – a universal assumption, that the church leader would be spending a significant amount of time with God. The people of God assumed that the leadership would be preaching, speaking to them and leading them out of a sustained encounter with God through the reading of Scripture, times of quiet and listening, and intercession on their behalf. The people of God still make this assumption, often crediting their leaders with much more than they should. The reality is a long way from this. Very many church leaders do not pray much on their own at all, often less than one hour per week.

My experience in these matters is within the Anglican Church supporting ordained leaders, a good amount of this in the evangelical part of this denomination. I have spoken with many ordained leaders who barely pray, but would not dream of telling their church members this. One male minister came to speak with me because he had not prayed on his own for over 20 years. The leader of an outwardly successful church, he would not dream of telling this to his church members or to those to whom he is accountable within the denomination. The drift away from a life rooted in prayer is accompanied by other signs of discontent and disappointment. Many enter ordained ministry with a very inflated view of themselves, often encouraged by friends and mentors. They have been told that they are a great preacher ('one of the best in my generation', one man told me), and they expect revival to come as part of their ministry. The size of the leadership task, the volume of work, and the expectations upon them become a burden too big to carry. Leaders learn quickly that they get the same results whether they pray or not. In fact, many learn that they can do very well indeed without prayer, not realizing that this is because of the gracious nature of God who is kind and generous to all, not just the minister concerned.

At Cranmer Hall each year we run a short conference for those who are about to leave to become curates, together with the vicars who will be their training incumbents. I like this training event very much. It is fun and positive, with all present carrying a good level of anticipation about what is ahead for these training partnerships. It is a fantastic privilege to be designated as the person to accompany another Christian leader as they begin public, paid, leadership ministry in the Church of England. The atmosphere is positive, and the vicars say all the right things and promise to do all that is required of them to enable this other minister to thrive. I consider these pairs of ministers, going out two-by-two reminding me of the mission in Luke's gospel, and wonder how they will fare. Within six months to a year several couples will be in trouble. There are two main reasons for this. The first is that although they promise otherwise some of these vicars will never pray with their curates, and some others might meet up just once per week but without much prayer taking place. This is far from sufficient to help a new minister going through the massive transition into ordained ministry in the Church of England, considering that the curate has promised to maintain a ministry-long pattern of daily prayer when they were ordained. The second main reason for failure is that male vicars are often threatened by the gifts and abilities of, as it happens, very able women curates. These women have to hold themselves in, hold back their gifts, rather than threaten their male colleagues. Lack of companionship in prayer and reduced space to offer gifts are key factors in the undermining of the confidence of young and gifted ministers.

So church leaders who began with passion and excitement can seem, all too soon, tired and dispirited. A good many leave full-time paid ministry after around five to 10 years. Many more stay because they have been de-skilled and have nowhere else to go, there is nothing else they can do. Those that stay, but are not spiritually alive, can slip into practices through which they shipwreck themselves. To follow this old-fashioned metaphor through, they have no anchor to hold them. Time spent in the study, which they might present as reading, prayer or preparation, might just as easily be time spent playing computer games, shopping or visiting sex sites. Feeling they are being required to give too much it can seem that the denomination or God 'owes' them something. Seen from this perspective fraud, theft, bullying or using people in some other way can be a kind of 'dues'. When it comes to this pattern of behaviours, whether as a leader or as a disciple, the Christian adult has lost the plot and forgotten both their call and their commission.

Finally, we do need to note that those that lead from the very edge of Church, from the margins where risk and experiment are greatest, can be those that are amongst the most vulnerable to breakdown, reckless sin and depression. This is a complex area, but there is good evidence to show that many come into Christian leadership after a profound and life-changing experience of grace. An individual who was living beyond the edge, but who experiences being found there by God, might then have a particular passion that others experience that same saving power. Such a Christian leader might be extremely persuasive in raising resources for mission into territory which is familiar to themselves, but not to the churches. The churches, from their perspective, can be blinded by the salvation story, and the person and the project can too easily become a trophy, a radical mark of God's special blessing upon them all. Very great care needs to be taken before such leaders are released, not least in checking that the whole spiritual life is in order, rooted in Christ and well disciplined. I am saddened to say, as someone at the heart of the Anglican evangelism and church planting movement of the 1980s and 1990s, that I know too many sad stories in this category. The damage done has harmed individual leaders, their families, and those that formed their Christian communities, as well as all those that followed them.

Raising up age-old foundations

So, is something new required? Do our times require a new approach, a newly shaped spirituality? It is clear that there are many now who, although they give lip-service to inherited models of spirituality, have drifted a long way from right practice. Inherited models of spirituality are associated with the Church in maintenance mode, and both can be dismissed together – is this wise? Would it not be better to shape contemporary spirituality around the shape and business of life today, would this not be more realistic? Pragmatically, better a spirituality that people live than one where they pretend.

I am not convinced, rather I would advocate a return to the 'age-old foundations', with a reassessment in the light of the demands on the leaders in the churches today. To throw away all that Christians have learnt in the presence of the Spirit over two thousand years seems more than a little reckless, and buys into the half-truth that no generation has been through such changing times as this one. I am also not convinced by the postmodern pick-and-mix spiritualities of the 1990s and early 2000s, where through an eclectic borrowing from the past all kinds of spiritual bits and pieces are cobbled together to make a kind of spiritual theme park that one can pass through. Nothing in itself is bad, but a constant moving on for new and different experiences does not encourage the kind of deep foundations or deep roots that are needed to sustain the demands of leadership ministry today, especially one in which the leader might take risks.

What do we get if we look at our inheritance? Well, we get a spirituality which is suited for discipleship, and this must be right because leaders are disciples first of all. What marks out the spirituality of the leader is the knowledge that much, maybe even all, of it should be open to view, to scrutiny. Leadership is a public function in the church, it is not hidden the way that other ministries (for example, intercession) might be. The leader is an exemplar for the community of disciples and to those that are of other faiths or no faith. This is a high calling indeed, but this too is at it should be, for a leader is trusted with a great deal. From those to whom much is given, much is expected.

Finally the requirements for the spirituality of leadership are obvious. We know that to keep our bodies healthy we must eat sensibly and exercise regularly. We understand that there is no way around this, and the older we get the more we realize the truth of this. The churches need young, passionate leaders who know how to keep themselves spiritually well for the long term, leaders who can last the distance, because these trying times of profound change will last the whole of our lives and beyond.

Marks of spirituality of leadership

1. A pattern of prayer woven through the whole of life

In the gospels we get a pretty good description of the pattern of prayer and worship of Jesus' life, and of the lives of his early followers. Jesus prayed regularly with other people, in the synagogues, in homes, in the streets and meeting places. Some of these prayers were formal, patterned expected prayers and blessings, the prayers that ran through the Judaism of his day. Other prayers were extempore, prompted by the circumstances and situations Jesus found himself in. The churches have maintained these traditions of formal prayers and extempore prayers, sometimes preferring one type over the other. However they meet different needs and fulfil different functions. At one time the place where these things were learnt was within the family home, but now they need to be carried over into the extended families and loose networks that make up the fabric of contemporary life. It is a delight to me when student ministers in Durham, living in households together, develop a natural shared life of prayer that marks out the times and the days, speaking of God's Lordship over all.

Alongside this pattern of prayer in life, Jesus participated in the custom of pilgrimage to Jerusalem, to mark the major festivals. The gospels record the number and purpose of these journeys differently, but in Luke as a child and as an adult Jesus makes a devotional journey to Jerusalem. Again this pattern of holy journeys, to Jerusalem, Rome, Canterbury, or to local holy places, made in the company of other pilgrims has passed down in the history of the churches. These were public journeys and acts of witness, acting as social levellers. They were costly in time and resources, and required the pilgrim to leave home in a profound way. Holidays in the Holy Land or the summer trip to New Wine are not the same thing at all. Marches of social protest and of prayer and penitence, as seen with the anti-slavery marches of 2007 might be closer in spirit. I think that this strand of Christian spirituality takes prayer out of our homes and churches and into the streets and public places.

Finally, Jesus sought out personal times of prayer alone. The gospels record his struggle to pray alone, and his need to pray more as demands on him increased. Having noted that it is in this area that so many leaders struggle it might be tempting to try to reconfigure prayer so we pray less alone and more together. It may be that we are not praying enough together, but it is difficult to imagine that we have come to times when we might now lay aside Jesus' directions to 'go into a room by yourself, shut the door, and pray to your Father'. Maybe the key to this is for each person to find a model of praying alone that works for them. And for this, as well as for the development of other aspects of personal and community prayer, the leader needs personal support and advice.

2. *A network of supportive relationships*

In most churches and denominations there is some sort of episcope or oversight offered through form of eldership where the ministry of a leader is made accountable and open to scrutiny. This is at the same time reassuring and threatening, welcomed and avoided, by ministers in leadership. To some degree this is because the ministry or work 'product' for the leader is 'church', and there is such a huge personal investment in ministry that critique of it can only ever be careful and gentle, or ministers in leadership crumple. This means that for much of the time it is very difficult indeed for any leader to really know the truth about themselves. If the review and accountability structures don't deliver truth, where else might a leader look for help?

Roy Oswald of the Alban Institute has engaged in much helpful work relating to the deployment of leaders in their first posts.[2] He has been able to identify four key roles that should be filled with respect to the new leader, if that person is going to thrive and steward themselves well in their new responsibility. He lists these four key relationships as: mentor, colleague, friend, and role model. The mentor is someone who has an overview of the post and responsibilities, who can help the minister set achievable targets and ministerial development outcomes. It is important to have a person who is truly a colleague, one who shares the load and provides spiritual and ministerial company. The friend is most usually a peer, doing the same or similar job in another place, one with whom tales can be told without a sense of judgement. Finally the minister needs a role model, someone who is exemplary and respected, who has walked a similar path before. Clearly, one person could carry more than one of these towards the minister, although it would be unusual for one person to be all four for another. Women ministers rarely find people to fill all four roles, as do pioneer ministers. The most difficult in each case is locating appropriate role models.

To these four significant roles I would add another, that of spiritual director. That is, a person who will help the leader examine their prayer life, someone who might know of a variety of resources that would enable a person under pressure to remain in a place of prayer, alone with God. It does seem vital to me that in a world of increasing busyness and instant communication, that there are leaders who are doing the counter-cultural activity of being still and listening to God. Those that can enable this counter-cultural activity are a scarce resource in the Church, one that is not much used or well developed in the evangelical tradition, but their time has come.

3. Reading Scripture and being read by it

The low level of biblical literacy of the people of God distresses many of us that work in theological education. It is one thing for those of no faith not to know the Bible, but it is quite another when evangelical students write assignments, preach sermons, make ethical decisions, and generally live their lives in a way that shows little acquaintance with or knowledge of Holy Scripture. If anything theological educators can exacerbate the problem. Those who have some working knowledge of some parts of Scripture when they begin leadership training are set back by their biblical studies at a course or college because they learn about the complexities and problems of the text, without being helped to a hermeneutic framework that holds them to the text. Even worse, a serious dissonance can emerge when the Bible is read in one way in class, but used in another way in the churches. In this way mature people can become post-biblical very quickly. This means that resources need to be invested in supporting leaders in the study of biblical hermeneutics, so that they remain not only readers of the text, but learn what it means to have one's life as a minister read by the text, questioned by it in profound ways. This kind of dialectic requires high levels of skill, but this should not surprise us. We know we live in complex times, so surely reading Scripture in these times will not be easy. What it does require, again, is an investment of quality time by the minister. For many the quick rewards in ministry that come through busyness will win over this one every time.

4. Support in transition

Many people are literally lost in translation, in the movement from one place to another, the movement from one time of life to another. Changes that are longed for and prayed for can bring significant disruption to a person. Those who knew who they were and how their world worked in one place may soon be lost in another. The Alban Institute points out that it is a common feature in transition for the minister to try to re-locate the past in the new place. Often this is done by reproducing a programme that worked elsewhere, rather than paying close attention to what is needed in the particular demands of the new place. Sometimes a minister will import people from their last place or network, to show those in the new place how things could be done, without thinking through what this might be read as saying to those who are constantly present in the new location.

More significantly than this, even for a minister who understands the pattern of transitional emotions, and has a good sense of who has good self-understanding, identity and call, there might be something in the new that resonates deeply within. This could be for good or ill, but will only be understood with support and help. Such support might come from good-quality theological supervision provided by someone from outside the setting, or sometimes the best understanding will come through therapeutic support. Again, these things take time and resources. It is my experience, personal and otherwise, that the learning in times of transition gives back a massive yield on investment.

When such prompts for learning and growth are ignored or not noticed a leader may over-invest, take on more than is necessary, not properly assess resources required or risk involved. The investment can be justified in terms of a faith adventure, the risk argued for in missional terms. When burnout follows, or a profound period of conflict, in which the leader does not feel supported by the wider denomination of the Church, then the natural reaction of many is to leave paid ministry. This has been one of the main reasons sited in the Duke research on ministers.[3]

5. *Giving and service at the heart of leadership*

Leadership involves the exertion of power and authority. This can be hugely costly, creating the impression that something is owed to the leader, or so seductive that the ego of the leader becomes inflated. Even more than this, Emerging Church leaders have to operate more and more beyond their authority, into networks and out of allegiances and transitory partnerships. I have commented above on the consequences of these feelings that emerge in such circumstances. What then can be done to guard the soul? How does a person stay holy? The answer, I think, lies in giving and service.

There is something very human about exerting power and then immediately wanting more. We see this in leaders in business and in politics, how hard it is not to take more, want more. This seductive loop is subverted by giving and by service. For this reason it is essential that the leaders in any Christian place do mundane jobs – wash cups, move chairs, or tidy up for example. This is seen occasionally, but not as much as you would expect. It is a double dilemma for women leaders, if the antidote to the seduction of power is service, how can a woman serve (wash up, say!) without falling back into traditional roles and expectations?

Jesus takes us to the heart of this in his understanding of the relationship of hospitality and the kingdom. It is the poor, the unworthy, the uninvited that he seeks to bring to table. In Luke's gospel he moves away from notions of what is deserved, and who should be included, to begin with those at the bottom of the pile in the human hierarchy. I think this means that the leader needs to notice who would be included naturally, and who would be excluded, and make a conscious move towards the excluded. As the leader often sets the agenda for inclusion and exclusion in a Christian community, it will mean paying great attention to internal inclinations towards influence, affluence and benefits, and in heart prayer and giving, moving in the other direction. Denominations will have different local struggles here, but for those in the Church of England, where the centre of gravity for leaders is located towards those with influence and prestige, resisting this gravitation force becomes vital if the leader's soul is to remain healthy.

6. *Knowing who you are, today, in Christ*

As disciples called to follow Jesus on the way all we can ever do is offer ourselves daily to God – or maybe as much as we understand about ourselves to as much as we understand of God. There is something about this at the end of 1 Corinthians 13, where Paul notices his own growth, and with it a changed understanding of God. We recognize that our knowledge is always partial, incomplete, but knowing who we are in Christ is deep and empowering knowledge for us all.

In John's gospel it is chapter 13 when Jesus knows who he is and what the Father has entrusted to him, knowing where he has come from, and when he is confident that he will return to God, that he is able to take a towel and engage in an act of service which is at the same time practical and profound. We need to encourage today's emerging leaders to this type of self-knowledge, which comes I believe through an open and accountable spiritual life. In this is both safety and blessing, for the minister and for the people of God.

Bibliography

Hodge, D.R., and J.E. Wenger, *Pastors in Transition: Why Clergy Leave Local Church Ministry* (Grand Rapids, MI: Eerdmans, 2005).

Oswald, Roy, 'Crossing the Boundary between Seminary and Parish', Alban OL122, (2007).

Notes

1. 'Those from among you will rebuild the ancient ruins; You will raise up the age-old foundations; And you will be called the repairer of the breach, The restorer of the streets in which to dwell' (Is. 58:12, American Standard Bible).
2. Oswald, Roy, 'Crossing the Boundary between Seminary and Parish', Alban OL122, (2007) See also www.alban.org.
3. Hodge, D.R., and J.E Wenger, *Pastors in Transition: Why Clergy Leave Local Church Ministry* (Grand Rapids, MI: Eerdmans 2005).

11

Turning the Corner: Educating the Theological Educators, Shaping Church Traditions and Engaging a New Generation

Rev Dr David Wilkinson

A footballer of an earlier generation and sometime manager of Newcastle United and England, Kevin Keegan, once said, 'I know what is around the corner ... but I'm not sure where the corner is'. The previous chapters in this book have ably painted a picture of what the future needs to address and given some models of what that future may be like. It is a remarkable collection spanning different generations, denominations and theological convictions. Yet in such diversity it is even more remarkable that there is such a lot of common ground, not least in the basic sense that something needs to be done if our traditional structures for training men and women for church leadership are going to connect with the emerging generations.

Yet how do we turn the corner and begin to head in a different direction? What are the challenges for those who lead denominations or groups of churches and for those who teach and train future church leaders? I write as a Methodist minister who is Principal of a college in Durham University which has within it men and women training for both Anglican and Methodist ordination. Not only am I responsible to the denominations for the kind of training we offer, I also teach courses in preaching and apologetics and so experience first hand the challenges of nurturing individuals in mission and ministry. I also write as someone who in his mid-40s feels between the 'generations' discussed in this book, that is a generation of young leaders emerging in a post-Christian culture and a generation of older leaders who have experienced something of the complexity of the decline of Christendom in the West.

I do believe that we can turn the corner, if we respond seriously to the challenges.

Being honest about where we are: a great disconnection or limited connectivity?

We have a wireless network in our home. It is a wonder of technology! I can collect email while waiting in the kitchen as the sausages grill and explore a topic on the web while the rest of the people in the lounge enjoy Strictly Come Dancing. However, in the small bedroom where I have a desk, and where I often want to do some work, I occasionally get a message saying 'limited connectivity'. I am told it is something to do with the thickness of walls and floor, but its erratic appearance seems to have more to do with high pressure over the North Sea.

Limited connectivity is more frustrating than no connection at all. It lulls you into believing that if you just wait and keep pressing the buttons on the keyboard, the information superhighway will return.

Now at this point I have a slight disagreement with my friend Rob Frost. I am not convinced that there is a great disconnection between young leaders and the theological training and formation offered through colleges and courses. That is not to diminish the seriousness of the situation we face. Some leaders called by God are damaged by the testing of a call, some are frustrated and deskilled by the college or course environment, and some are forced out of their church traditions into parachurch ministries. However some are not. Not all of the young generation of leaders are the same. Some have grown through the testing of a call, some have flourished in training and some are now exercising ministries of considerable influence within their denominations.

My own experience here in Durham is that we have seen some outstanding young leaders grow and develop, indeed one of these young leaders is the author of one of the chapters of this book and a co-editor. Further, many of the suggestions concerning the future of leadership training made in this book are already standard practice – courses are flexible both in their delivery and learning styles; we do strive for the best combination of knowledge, understanding, skills and character formation; we are in constant dialogue with churches concerning the kind of leaders they want and need; assessment is no longer just the essay but can take the form of structured conversations, multi-media projects, theological reflection on sermons or pastoral encounters, book proposals, cell group outlines and radio scripts. All of this takes place in courses shared by Anglican, Methodist and Roman Catholic colleges and all are validated by the rigorous high academic standards of Durham University. Similar stories can be told in many other places.

However, limited connectivity is much more dangerous than a great disconnection. The fact that we are making progress in theological training by incorporating recent insights from business and higher education, creating diversity and recognizing the value of younger leaders, should not lull us into believing that all will be well. The average age of those coming into training is far too high and the small percentage of leaders under the age of 40 within the main denominations is not only a cause of concern for the long-term future of the Church but is also a sad denial of skills and energy for the Church of today.

Limited connectivity may mean that we have not done enough to communicate this new environment of theological training to the young leaders of this generation, or indeed to those older leaders who mentor them and convey a college experience of decades ago. There is a real task of communication here. At the same time we cannot ignore that we must reform our training and nurture even more in the light of what God is doing in our culture and our context.

Limited connectivity is dangerous because it encourages you to fiddle in optimism rather than take decisive action in the energy of Christian hope. The way to deal with it is for you to recognize the problem, recognize its seriousness and do something about it. The concerns raised in this book need to be taken seriously by colleges and courses, denominational leaders and in the expectations of local churches.

Returning to our roots

The questions and concerns of this book are not unique. As Cracknell has highlighted, the second generation of Methodist preachers on both sides of the Atlantic opposed the need for formal theological education.[1] Early Methodist preachers, such as Francis Asbury or Hugh Bourne, were often self-taught and found themselves in conflict with university-trained clergy. As their ministries were blessed by God many found themselves asking why did preachers and evangelists need such education? Cracknell argues that underneath this was a pervasive anti-intellectualism as a result of the tendency to exalt personal experience at the expense of everything else. Anti-intellectualism remains a factor today. This has been a reaction against an exaltation of intellectualism in theological formation. It has also been due to a subtle identification of the role of the intellect in theology with liberal or anti-charismatic traditions.

One of the most important ways of dealing with this is to go back to our common roots within scripture. For example in Acts 20:17–38 we have a very powerful picture of Paul and the young leaders of the church in Ephesus. They may not have been young in age, but they were young in experience. This is Paul's farewell address as he makes his way to Jerusalem for Pentecost. He has limited time so he calls the elders of the church to meet him at Miletus. There he speaks of what is ahead and using himself as a model for their leadership, he looks back over his own ministry.

First, we notice the importance of *the theological educator as role model*. Paul in fact appeals to their experience of his life and ministry as something that allows them to trust his direction, teaching and advice (vv. 18–19). Paul was a practitioner and a teacher and indeed did not see the distinction. In a world of theological education where PhDs are increasingly standard for appointments to teach, there is a real danger that theological colleges and courses are staffed by those who have little experience of ministry, mission and leadership. Of course, very few tutors or mentors will encompass both the depth of experience and academic achievement, but this in itself emphasizes the importance of building teams of those who will form the next generation for ministry. The nature of these teams needs to be much more flexible and dynamic. The concept of the staff of a theological college being a constant group of people who have been teaching in that place for over a decade can no longer work. Teams will constantly be changing as some come in from ministry to teach for a few years and then return to wider ministry. A smaller core team of tutors will co-ordinate networks of specialists from the Church and the academic world who will educate, mentor and pastor those who are being formed for ministry.

It is important that theological educators are role models not just in thinking, or ministry but also in holy living. Paul was no detached professional. He taught not only publicly but also house to house (v. 20). It is also clear that there was a deep emotional bond between Paul and his leaders (vv. 37–8), and while time was short he still found time to pray with them (v. 36).

Second, Paul shows *an extraordinary affirmation of the call of these leaders*. He tells them that the Holy Spirit 'has made you overseers, to shepherd the church of God' (v. 28). Barrett calls this the theological and practical centre of the speech, pointing out that Paul uses the same language here as for his own call.[2] Affirmation then leads to responsibility. Today in assessing a call we have perhaps tended to an atmosphere of testing to the expense of affirmation. The long process in the Methodist Church of candidating through the questioning of many committees, or the reporting structure to assess Anglican ordinands while at college or on courses can quite easily lead to a sense of hurdles to be jumped rather than a sense of common discernment. We need to move beyond the 'them' and 'us' model of teacher and student, to a model of shared dependency in learning based on the model of the body of Christ. On a number of occasions throughout this book the model of Jesus and his disciples is helpfully used. Can we use that to shape our structures rather than simply paying it lip service?

Third, Paul models *the necessity of biblical and theological depth*. He proclaimed (v. 20, v. 25), taught (v. 20), testified (v. 21, v. 24), declared (v. 27), and warned (v. 31) the Ephesians. He shared with them 'the message' (v. 20), 'repentance and faith' (v. 21), 'the good news of God's grace' (v. 24), 'the kingdom' (v. 25), 'the whole purpose of God' (v. 27), 'the message of his grace' (v. 32). It is interesting that he stresses that he did this both 'publicly and from house to house' (v. 20). In fact if we go back to the record of Paul in Ephesus in Acts 19:1–20 we see a little of what this means. For three months he spoke out boldly and argued persuasively in the synagogue (Acts 19:8) and then for two years daily in the lecture hall of Tyrannus (Acts 19:9). This could not have been an easy experience. I may be pushing the picture a little too far, but it does speak to me of the importance of doing theological education in the public square as well as within the Christian community. Theological depth is developed both in the safe environment of encouraging fellow Christians and in the aggressive and challenging environment of other worldviews and assumptions. There is a place therefore for both the Bible college and the university college in theological formation. We need as churches to maintain this diversity. Not all training courses and colleges need to be validated by university departments. At the same time, some colleges need to continue to be open to the scrutiny and educational structures of secular universities. Christian leadership formation must be committed to equipping the leader as the 'theological consultant' for a local church, and this takes time.

Further, some of those leaders need to push the theological questions to a greater depth if the move of God's Spirit is going to bear fruit in the long term. Richard Lovelace saw this clearly in terms of the history of movements of the Spirit within the Great Awakenings. He wrote, 'The purity of a revival is intimately related to its theological substance. Unless revival involves and issues in theological reformation its energy will be contained and its fruit will not last'.[3] This is especially the case of resisting those ideas and individuals who will come as savage wolves (v. 29) or distorters of truth (v. 30). If, as I believe, this new generation of leaders is going to flourish then they must be equipped to discern the dangers both inside and outside of the Church. This is far more than a confrontational style of theological training which is intended to equip people to sniff out heresy and publicly condemn it. The encouragement to 'be on your guard' (v. 31) is not the Christian equivalent of the British soldier in bearskin and dress uniform standing unmoving on the streets of London. This is much more dynamic. It involves being alert and watching over yourselves (v. 28). Here a strong rhythm of prayer, Bible reading, confession and corporate worship is essential in the theological formation of the leader. While the Anglican tradition of morning and evening prayer can be dismissed too easily for its churchiness, it provides a rhythm of encountering scripture daily and indeed large parts of scripture if it is done properly. There is great value in the common prayer of a college community or a dispersed course in building the foundations of ministry. It is far too easy in the success or failure of ministry to lose real engagement with scripture and prayer. Paul is arguing that only if the elders remained faithful to God would their congregations remain faithful. Billy Graham, in all the success of his ministry, kept asking the question, 'have I been faithful to what God has called me to do?'

Fourth, Paul *inspires a vision which is universal and transforming*. Verse 21 is a very simple picture of ministry as Paul says he 'testified to both Jews and Greeks about repentance towards God and faith towards our Lord Jesus'. Yet it is a profound vision. It is not limited by ethnic, cultural or historic boundaries and it is about lives changed and transformed. While the mantra of the missionary movement of the early twentieth century to convert the world within a generation may have been naïve and arrogant, it does seem to me that we are in danger of going to the opposite extreme. Too often the selection and training of church leaders fails to rise above the details to see the big vision. Further, our desire is to form leaders as 'safe pairs of hands' rather than those who will take risks, cross boundaries and have faith that God will transform people and communities. Young leaders come with both naïve optimism and big visions. How do we bring reality to the optimism and yet affirm the vision? An obvious answer is to hear the stories of those who have seen God at work and within the reality and struggle of ministry keep a big vision. Fundamental to my own ministry was the time on student placement with the co-editor of this book. Rob Frost inspired countless young leaders including myself, not by his theological ingenuity or, it has to be said, by his dress sense, but by his large vision of what God can do. So student placements, invited preachers, theological college and course staff need to inspire a vision which is universal and transforming. Theological formation too often has the feel of undermining rather than the feel of celebration.

Fifth, *leadership is characterized by sacrifice and grace.* Paul is on the way to Jerusalem, the way of imprisonments and persecutions (vv. 22–3). He has endured trials (v. 19) and will now be permanently separated from his friends at Ephesus. While ministering among them he supported himself and his ministry team through hard work (vv. 33–4). This is a long way from the comfortable nature and high expectations of ministry in Western culture. With respect to my younger friends, I see in some of them the rhetoric of sacrifice but an approach to ministry which is dominated by a culture of consumerism and rights. I see it in them because I see it in myself. It is a very easy trap to fall into – me and my gifts, me and my church, me and my calling. I want and often think I deserve a chance on the big platforms, a lifestyle which marks out how special my gifts are, and a church which owes me a debt of gratitude. Yet Paul lived a lifestyle which embodied sacrifice and grace. It came from his deep sense of call and gratitude for what God had done. He faces sacrifice because he is captive to the leading of the Spirit (v. 22) and sees his own life in comparison 'with the task of finishing the race and testifying to the gospel of God's grace' (v. 24).

I remember this being brought home to me in a most profound way when I was beginning as a young leader. Alan Redpath was pastor at the Moody Memorial Church in Chicago and then at Charlotte Baptist Church in Edinburgh. It was then that a cerebral stroke forced him to retire but he found an international role in speaking and teaching. He often came to speak at our university Christian Union. I remember one evening in particular when before he started to read the bible passage, he said, 'I want to testify that my life was changed during your Annual General Meeting last year'. I have to say that I have not known a lot of people changed by an Annual General Meeting, so my interest was caught. He continued to explain. He and his wife had been living in the grounds of a lovely Bible school and life was great. The previous year he had come to the CU to speak but had found that before his talk was the short annual meeting with reports given by the officers. The 20-year-old President gave a report in which he made the observation that he felt many of today's students had lost the element of sacrifice in their Christian lives. Alan Redpath said that God had taken that word and pushed it deep into his heart and mind. He began to realize that life was very nice, but where was the sacrifice? He went home and prayed it over with his wife. Some months later they decided to move to Birmingham to a block of flats in order to witness to and serve others.

Now of course this calling to a life of sacrifice is not an excuse for church communities not to look after their own leaders properly and generously, and for church leaders to neglect their families or their own physical and mental needs. Nor is it to be used as a mental justification of salvation by works or how to impress your co-workers with just how sacrificial you are. Theological formation needs to use the stories and models of sacrificial living carefully and wisely. For many students, particularly those who by their gender, race or age are discriminated against and find themselves dominated by structures of serving others, then the language of sacrifice can be used to legitimize something that is wrong. Here the motive and limits of sacrificial living have to be carefully explored.

Paul brings an excitement and even joy to this subject. It is based on what Christ has done for him, the experience of the Spirit in his life and that the ministry he is called to is a ministry of grace. It is this grace into which Paul commends these young leaders (v. 32), for it is able to build them up and give them an inheritance. Howard Marshall comments that this is perhaps based on Deuteronomy 33:3, appearing to refer to God's gift of a share in the blessings of his kingly rule. This is not about forming leaders who are arrogant but leaders who are confident in being loved, called and empowered by God. Donald English used to say that every Christian should get up in the morning and the first thing they should say is 'Jesus died for me and I am loved'. The priority of the body of Christ is to help its leaders to know that they are justified by grace and not by the size of their ministry.

If sacrifice and grace characterize leadership, then they must also characterize the leadership of theological colleges and courses, and indeed the denominations or trusts who control them. It needs to be modelled in relationships between staff and students, and in a desire to build the Kingdom rather than an institution. One of the marks of this will be how we support the weak (v. 35).

Person-centred rather than programme-dictated

One of the extraordinary things about the biblical record of God's call to men and women as leaders is its diversity. It would be great fun to design a training course for some of these leaders. Perhaps 'Basic Eloquence and Rhetoric' for Moses, 'Pastoral Sensitivity' for Simon Peter, 'An introduction to the Holy Spirit' for Apollos and 'Dealing with a depressing situation' for Jeremiah! Women and men, young and old, Jew and Gentile are all called by God into a wide variety of callings in a wide variety of times and cultures. At the same time, as we have seen with the Ephesian elders and (earlier in the book) the formation of the disciples by Jesus, individual callings are shaped, nurtured and directed within community life and learning. Yet the pressures of denominational requirements and limited resources in training often mean that this celebration of diversity in community is severely limited.

Now of course there are never going to be unlimited resources to provide all the dreams of this book by next year. However I do think that there are certain attitudes within those responsible for training and theological formation that could help to connect with this emerging generation of leaders.

First, we need *to move beyond the 'student as a blank sheet of paper' approach.* This approach sees a student as bringing with them to training no skills, experience or gifts. They are simply then a blank sheet of paper which is ready to be filled by classes, seminars and workshops. Of course every training institution or course will deny that it uses such an approach, yet it is a consistent theme that I hear from students in training. The VOX research project on the teaching of preaching, apologetics and media literacy in more than 60 theological training colleges and courses asked whether staff used the experience and gifts of their students in the teaching of these areas. The vast majority replied no.[4] Yet students do have gifts and experience which must be used to enhance the learning experience. In my own theological college I have taught a class on evangelistic preaching which had one of Billy Graham's senior advisors, a class on media relations which had senior press officers, and a class on youth culture which had most of the class knowing more about youth ministry than me! Flexible pathways of training which build on people's past experiences and gifts, collaborative learning and teaching between staff and students, and a humility shown by staff are not only good educational approaches, they also help the young leader feel affirmed rather than de-skilled.

Indeed, do we need to move beyond the language of 'student' and 'staff', or the power structures associated with them? I recall at a conference coffee time, sitting down beside a young woman training for ordination at a UK institution and asking her how she was doing. She burst into tears. Somewhat surprised I asked her why and she replied, 'No member of staff has asked me that in 18 months of training and no member of staff has ever sat with me on the same level'. I am sure this extreme reaction was unusual, but it constantly acts as a reminder to me of how we style teaching and learning. A number of us have found great resources in the model of coaching.[5] The models of mentoring, discipling and inter-dependence in the body of Christ need to supplement and shape the models of student and teacher.

Second, we need *to be continually exploring the nature of vocation*. Within the traditional denominations the default model saw a church leader who comes into college training after a first degree at university, who will give 40 years of ministry to the Church, and will be supported by a wife who is very good at making scones! Now of course we have moved a long way from that. Or have we? Recognizing the call of God upon women as well as men to church leadership has been a great joy of the past decades, but there will be many women who rightly say that the values and models of training still reflect the men who remain in control of such structures. While the Church's theological understanding of ordination may stress the commitment for life, the changing circumstances of our culture may need to nuance that afresh. In a post-Christian culture, where the church may not have the resources to support full-time life-long ministry, or in a 'liquid church' where ministries need to be much more flexible and short-term, we need different models for young people which do not lessen the commitment but work with the way they see a dynamic God at work in very different and rapidly moving culture.

Third, we need *to pay as much attention to the prophet as to the pastor or priest*. Again, theological understandings would say that all these three things are important in forming leaders. However, pastors and priests are usually very safe, while prophets are very risky. I wonder how many of our training courses would have been able to cope with Ezekiel for example! Let us rejoice in creative people and people who are a pain to the institution, whether in theology, practice or personality. There is often a subtle pressure that potential leaders should be a 'safe pair of hands' and this extends not only to training requirements but also to selection requirements. While of course all leaders need to be responsible in both doctrine and practice of leadership and training is about equipping them to do that, the Church in western Europe needs leaders who, in the words of John Pritchard, will be 'mature risk-takers',[6] who will see new visions and who will be prophetic voices both to the body of Christ and to culture.

Thus training programmes need to move beyond just an induction into an institution had to be characterized by prophetic engagement. Apologetics and preaching need as much time and space as counselling skills and liturgy. At a much more important level, there are real questions for any curriculum about the place for missiology and practical theology in colleges and courses. Practical or applied theology is not about practical tips on ministry, but is about taking the context that God has given us seriously. That is, we need to do our theology having worked hard at analysing and understanding the world around us, and then to see our theology as contributing to the world becoming what God intends it to be.[7] Likewise, missiology is not just teaching tips on evangelism, but a way of looking at all theological questions from the point of view of the theology of mission which takes what God is doing in different cultures seriously.

In addition, it will mean a commitment to seeing leadership within a much bigger vision of the body of Christ. Within the Methodist church, the Circuit system can bring together a number of ordained leaders and churches into a structure for local ministry and mission. Yet few Circuits allow their ministers to develop different gifts or areas of expertise in any meaningful way. Can we have a big vision that sees the training and deployment of leaders not in a model which sees the local church and its pastor as a 'jack of all trades' but as the local church and its leaders as part of the body of Christ? What then does it mean to see training and deployment across the churches, and across both the ordained and the laity?

Fourth, we need *to provide a context where passion is nurtured in compassion.* Albert Outler, the Methodist historian, explored the movement of John Wesley from harsh critic to sympathetic pastor. Outler argued that the key point for Wesley was his experience of field preaching on 2 April 1739 and the subsequent change where 'his passion for truth had been transformed into compassion for persons'.[8] If leadership emerges out of passion, the Church must first recognize and rejoice in it. It then needs to give a learning context and learning opportunities where leaders deepen their compassion for those in need. This is the foundation for servant leadership in the model of Jesus.

Croft and Walton offer the biblical pictures of journey, parenting, agriculture and building for Christian growth and development and argue that these images are at the heart of what it means to be a Christian minister.[9] However in a Western culture which views journey, agriculture and building in a very impersonal way, we need to recapture the biblical vision of ministry stemming from compassion. Perhaps the parenting image is the one most needed in our models of training.

Fifth, we need *to use the gifts that God has given us to provide diversity and depth in training.* For a number of years I have been teaching a class in Christian apologetics to students living in the US while sat in my office in Durham. The whole module is done on the web and I have not met personally the majority of students. Not only does it open new possibilities of cross-cultural learning for ministry, it has also surprised me. The surprise is that the quality of theological reflection of my web-based students is far greater than my classroom students. This was completely counter-intuitive for me. I had thought that working with a group in the classroom was the best way and the web would be a second best. In fact, in learning for ministry, two things have worked against this assumption. The first is that people on the web course have more time and opportunity to contribute comments, questions and insights in the class discussion on a message board than by putting their hand in the air in a classroom. Indeed, for many, they never put their hand in the air. Second, many on the web course are doing their learning from real situations of work and ministry. Some come in on a Sunday evening after preaching to do some work on Christian communication. Some reflect immediately from their secular work on the way to build bridges for the gospel. Of course a virtual community has its limitations, but the new technologies of web-based learning, video-conferencing, social networking have much to give us in providing diversity that will address the problem of connectivity. At the same time models of mentoring, formation and learning from business and education have much to offer. The theological educators of the future do not all need PhDs in theology, but need to bring networks of people and ideas into the formation of church leaders.

This is an exciting time. The challenge of a new generation of leaders is one that can transform the Church. We need to be honest about our weaknesses, return to our roots and find new ways so that God's calling for each person can be brought to fruition. Max Warren, the distinguished missiologist, once wrote, 'I find this a most exciting moment to be alive. I want to fill what days remain to my lot to help folk to recover some basic certainties and then be ready to explore how to relate these certainties to a new world and a new age. The great days of mission lie ahead – Hallelujah'.[10]

Bibliography

Ballard, P. and J. Pritchard, *Practical Theology in Action: Christian Thinking in the Service of the Church and Society* (London: SPCK, 2006).

Croft, S. and R. Walton, *Learning for Ministry* (London: Church House, London, 2005).

Jervell, J. and W. Meeks, *God's Christ and His People* (Oslos: Universitetsforl, 1977).

Kings, G., *Christianity Connected: Hindus, Muslims and the World in the Letters of Max Warren and Roger Hooker* (Zoetermeer: Boekencentrum, 2002).

Lovelace, R. F., *Dynamics of Spiritual Life* (Leicester: InterVarsity Press, 1979).

Outler, A., *Evangelism in the Wesleyan Spirit* (Nashville, TN: Tidings, 1971).

Pritchard, J., *The Life and Work of a Priest* (London: SPCK, 2007).

Shaw, P. and R. Linnecar, *Business Coaching: Achieving Practical Results Through Effective Engagement* (Chichester: Capstone, 2007).

Notes

1. Cracknell, K., 'No Starts, False Starts and Fresh Starts' in *Theological Education Consultation, World Methodist Council*, Rio de Janeiro, General Board of Higher Education, The United Methodist Church, 1996, p. 14.

2. Barrett, C. K., 'Paul's address to the Ephesian Elders' in Jervell, J. and W. Meeks, *God's Christ and His People* (Oslos: Universitetsforl, 1977), 107–21.

3. Lovelace, R. F., *Dynamics of Spiritual Life* (Leicester: InterVarsity Press, 1979), 126.

4. Stevenson, G., *The VOX project 21st Century Communication: A Research Report on the Provision of Training in Preaching, Apologetics and Media* (Durham: Centre for Christian Communication, 2003).

5. Shaw, P. and R. Linnecar, *Business Coaching: Achieving Practical Results Through Effective Engagement* (Chichester: Capstone, 2007).

6. Pritchard, J., *The Life and Work of a Priest* (London: SPCK, 2007), 129.

7. Ballard, P. and J. Pritchard, *Practical Theology in Action: Christian Thinking in the Service of the Church and Society* (London: SPCK, 2006).

8. Outler, A., *Evangelism in the Wesleyan Spirit* (Nashville, TN: Tidings, 1971), 19.

9. Croft, S. and R. Walton, *Learning for Ministry* (London: Church House, 2005), 193.

10. Kings, G., *Christianity Connected: Hindus, Muslims and the World in the Letters of Max Warren and Roger Hooker* (Zoetermeer: Boekencentrum, 2002), 211.

Youthwork After Christendom

Jo and Nigel Pimlott

Young people have been leaving the church for several decades and are largely absent from many of our congregations. Many young people remain interested in spirituality but have no desire to embrace a church perceived as old fashioned. How can they be empowered to follow Jesus in a relevant and new way that is responsive to the challenges of the current context? By examining the influences of the past, exploring the stories of those young people who have been partaking in church and by considering the views of those not connected to Church, this book offers insights, theology, practical application and some hope for the future.

> 'Jo and Nigel don't duck any issues. Lucid, well argued, gritty and real, their book is a wake up call for the church and youth ministry – I hope we have ears to hear and courage to flesh out their vision.' – **Jonny Baker**, Mission Leadership and Communities Team leader with the Church Mission Society

Jo Pimlott is Assistant Director of the Midlands Centre for Youth Ministry based at St John's College, Nottingham. **Nigel Pimlott** is the co-ordinator of the Connect Spiritual Development Project and National Youth Work Development Advisor for Frontier Youth Trust.

978-1-84227-507-1

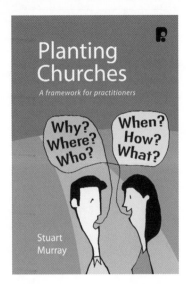

Planting Churches

A Framework for Practitioners

Stuart Murray

Who can be involved in church planting? Where should we plant new churches? What kinds of churches? How do we go about this? What resources do we need? What are the pitfalls? And is church planting still relevant in an era of fresh expressions and emerging churches? Stuart Murray draws on thirty years experience as a practitioner, trainer and consultant to address these and many other questions. *Planting Churches* explains why church planting is crucial if we are to incarnate the gospel in a changing culture and guides practitioners through the whole process of planting a new church.

> '*Planting Churches* is full of wisdom. It will rapidly become a standard text book on the subject for pioneers from a range of churches.' – **Steven Croft**, Archbishops' Missioner and Team Leader of Fresh Expressions

Stuart Murray is the founder of Urban Expression, a pioneering church planting agency.

978-1-84227-611-2